Untouched by the Conflict

Untouched by the Conflict

The Civil War Letters of Singleton Ashenfelter,

Dickinson College

Edited by Jonathan W. White and Daniel Glenn

THE KENT STATE UNIVERSITY PRESS ◼ KENT, OHIO

Frontispiece: Singleton M. Ashenfelter and Samuel W. Pennypacker (Courtesy of Pennypacker Mills, County of Montgomery, Schwenksville, PA)

For Paul S. Trible Jr.,

who has established Christopher Newport University

as a preeminent liberal arts university

Contents

Illustrations

J. MATTHEW GALLMAN

Foreword

THOSE OF US WHO STUDY THE CIVIL WAR, AND ESPECIALLY THE CIVIL War home front, love to wade into wartime diaries and letters. This is particularly true for historians who focus on life in the North. Civilians who wrote letters left us an invaluable account of a nation at war. Some correspondents penned long discussions of what they thought about the war. They wrote details about particular events; they recorded personal opinions about particular battles and campaigns; they captured immediate responses to conflicts and celebrations in their own communities. Others only mentioned the war's military and political narrative on rare occasions, providing the historian with a useful quote here and there. While this is partially just a reflection of what people chose to write about in their letters, it also illustrates a larger truth: in the Civil War North, many aspects of life carried on almost undisturbed by events on distant battlefields. Such was the reality of the Northern home front.

The wartime letters of Singleton Ashenfelter, a student at Dickinson College in Carlisle, Pennsylvania, are a great source about mid-nineteenth century America, particularly the Civil War home front. Readers looking for commentary on the war as a military and political struggle will find very few nuggets within this correspondence. In a broader sense one might argue that Ashenfelter's relative silence about such major events is in fact an eloquent commentary about the role of the national conflict in the daily lives of at least some civilians at home. If Ashenfelter—who was a young man during the war—was deeply concerned about the details of the conflict, he did not let those concerns sneak into his correspondence very often. Occasionally, one finds a comment on events important to the Civil War narrative. He wrote some useful letters about antiwar Democrats (he disliked them) and had a bit to say about the

Army of Northern Virginia's 1862 invasion of Maryland, which culminated in the Battle of Antietam (on September 17). But the truth is that, day in and day out, Singleton Ashenfelter devoted his fascinating letters to his own life and thoughts. And as a chronicler of such, he has provided the historian with invaluable information about a host of fairly elusive topics.

Let me suggest a few.

Ashenfelter's letters offer a marvelous window into the daily life of the mid-nineteenth-century college student. Historians have just begun to explore the collegiate worlds in both the North and the South. Some have asked questions about the impact of the Civil War on students' lives, while others have looked more broadly at the role of colleges and universities in shaping men and society. Ashenfelter's letters are rich with the quotidian details of a young man's world in these institutions. We learn about the rules that defined a man's life at Dickinson and the discipline that transgressors faced. Ashenfelter, who would describe himself as a "good fellow" more than a "good student," threw himself into club life and literary societies, even being tabbed to deliver a major address on "Religious Liberty." On occasion he got drawn into college hijinks, including one occasion when he posted a series of anonymous parodies on a Dickinson bulletin board, earning himself a bit of notoriety among his peers. Such accounts are priceless windows into wartime college life. Along the way we learn quite a bit about what Ashenfelter read and admired, about his classes, and about his thoughts on various teachers, authors, and ideas.

These comments about college life are interspersed with a wealth of information about the thoughts and personal preoccupations of a young man in midcentury America. In truth, many Civil War–era men—both at home or in uniform—were quite introspective about large ideas. But the range of topics that absorbed Ashenfelter's thoughts, not to mention the depth of his writings, is distinctive, even when the topics themselves are familiar. As a college student, Ashenfelter developed a strong affection for alcohol, an issue he periodically confronted and attempted to limit. Like many other young men, he wrestled with both religion and his own vices. Concluding that he could not believe in any "Deity," he nevertheless devoted many pages to discussions of organized religion. Looking in the mirror, Ashenfelter often seemed to find himself wanting, worried about his selfishness and sloth as well as his drinking and other misbehaviors. (He devotes one long paragraph to his unfortunate "habit of swearing.") And, like many other young men, Ashenfelter expended much thought and energy on young women. In the space of just a few years, he managed to grow deeply attached to at least three women, providing plenty of details about courtship, while also perpetually questioning his own impulses and actions. But around the age of twenty, Ashenfelter seems to have settled on Annie Euen as the principle object of his substantial desires, providing interesting insights about both friendship and courtship between young men and women during this period.

These are just a few of the many topics that come up in these letters. Having myself read many dozens of collections of wartime letters and diaries, much of Ashenfelter's introspection feels more like what one might find in a young man's diary, not in his correspondence with another man. If we step away from the individual passages and letters as bits of evidence and consider this book as a single fascinating document, it becomes—I think—a wonderful source for two interconnected themes: the nature of midcentury masculinity, and the shape and character of friendships among men.

This book is at its core a portrait of the intense friendship between Singleton Ashenfelter and Samuel Pennypacker as viewed through the lens of Ashenfelter's letters. Pennypacker was only a year older, but sometimes he seemed to adopt a mentor role. As the editors explain, the two men remained friends for a half century. This collection captures their relationship when they were still young, trying to navigate their futures.

These letters from "Sing" to "Pennie" include a surprising number of comments about the etiquette of correspondence and much more about the nature of friendship. Sing apologizes for being "dilatory" (February 12, 1863) in responding to Pennie's most recent missive. This becomes a recurring theme as letters carefully dissect who owes the next letter, with Sing periodically chafing at gaps between incoming correspondence. In late November 1863 he writes an extremely long letter to Pennie, confessing his loneliness at Dickinson and admitting, "I miss most just such a friend as I feel you to be." The college continued to provide pleasant distractions, but no friend had emerged on campus who could match the pleasures he enjoyed with Pennie. In this long letter Sing takes a lengthy digression to describe a classmate named Jackson, who he feels is a true "genius." "I am so deeply interested in this Jackson that I could not refrain from telling you of him," he admits. But it becomes clear that Sing is seeking not merely a kindred spirit in Jackson but a replacement for Pennie. "When I think of how often I would write to you if I only owed you a letter," he writes, "I feel as if I would like it better were we to drop all formality & write just when we feel inclined; without reference to answered or unanswered letters. Would such a correspondence suit you," he wondered (November 22, 1863). The following May Sing returns to these themes, declaring, "I wish I could find words to express my intense loneliness. I am not homesick, but friendsick." Having defined his classmate Jackson as an intriguing genius, Sing takes pains to describe "Sam" (Pennypacker) as a genius too in several subsequent letters.

There is much to unpack in this correspondence—or the half that we may now read—between Ashenfelter and Pennypacker; one is left to wonder if Sam's return letters were quite so long, introspective, and full of passion. Sing was only slightly younger, but at times he seems to look up to Sam as an object of admiration. Pennypacker had left school and moved on with his life to study law in Philadelphia, a path his friend would soon follow. Sing wrote to Sam on May 9, 1865, Ashenfelter's twenty-first birthday—an occasion of multiple transitions, his college career about to end and having begun preparations to embark on his own legal career. The previous month their mutual friend Horace Lloyd had married amid a swirl of controversy and bad feeling. (Ashenfelter disapproved of the match and did not mind saying so.) And Sing reveals that he has recently learned that Sam has been sending long letters to Alice Lee, which did not please him in the least. This letter—shorter than many of his earlier missives—also drifts to more praise of Jackson's literary abilities, tempered by thoughts on the young author's inability to remain sober. Then he turns abruptly to the end of the Civil War, praising Grant's victory but questioning Lincoln's leniency toward "the rebels." Ashenfelter closes with cryptic comments about Lloyd's marriage and his own relationship with "Miss Sue." Such was the complex world of a highly literate young man turning twenty-one only weeks after the Civil War ended.

Acknowledgments

THIS PROJECT COULD NOT HAVE BEEN COMPLETED WITHOUT THE generous support of several people and institutions. Bill Blair and the George and Ann Richards Civil War Era Center at Penn State funded a summer research fellowship for Jonathan White at Pennypacker Mills in the summer of 2000, when he first encountered Ashenfelter's letters. Elizabeth and Nathan Busch, codirectors of Christopher Newport University's Center for American Studies, funded much of Daniel Glenn's time working on this project. An Andrew W. Mellon Fellowship supported White's research on Dickinson College at the Virginia Museum of History and Culture. A Faculty Development Grant from Christopher Newport University, funded by Provost Dave Doughty, and professional-development funds from the Department of Leadership and American Studies, supported a research trip to Pennypacker Mills as well as other aspects of the research for this volume. Glenn received grants from the Honors Program and the Undergraduate and Graduate Research Council, which helped defray costs related to publishing the book. Our thanks to Jay Paul and David Salomon for this support.

Matt Gallman and Michael David Cohen both read the manuscript with keen eyes and offered extraordinarily helpful suggestions for improving the book. Will Underwood of Kent State University Press has been a wonderful supporter of this project, and we are grateful for his time and expertise. Kevin Brock did an excellent job copyediting the manuscript. Finally, we thank Mike Gray for helping us think through this project in its early stages.

We thank Carl Klase of Pennypacker Mills and Jim Gerencser of the Dickinson College Archives and Special Collections for their generosity and assistance as we worked on Ashenfelter's letters. Both answered numerous questions by email, phone, and in person. Jasmine Smith, Margaret Baillie, and Pamela Powell of the Chester County Historical Society helped us locate useful information and photographs. Christopher Newport University's interlibrary-loan specialist, Jesse Spencer, tracked down a number of items for us that facilitated our research. We are grateful to Pennypacker Mills and Montgomery County, Pennsylvania, for permission to reproduce these letters as well as to Dickinson College for permission to reproduce the letter in Appendix C and the speech in Appendix D.

Note on Method

THIS VOLUME REPRODUCES UNABRIDGED TRANSCRIPTIONS OF ALL OF Singleton Ashenfelter's letters to Samuel Pennypacker from 1862 until just after Ashenfelter's graduation from Dickinson College in 1865. Pennypacker's responses do not appear to have survived. We have striven to keep Ashenfelter's writing as close to the originals as possible. In a few instances we have created new paragraph breaks to assist readers through longer paragraphs that cover multiple pages and topics. Where letters were scrunched together, we have given him the benefit of the doubt and rendered words with correct spellings; however, all obvious spelling errors have been retained except in a few instances where we inserted missing letters, words, or punctuation in brackets to provide clarity for the reader. We silently deleted many of Ashenfelter's superfluous commas, with the exception of those in his letter of September 28, 1862, which requires the extra commas to convey the humorous pacing of his writing. Words that could not be deciphered are either marked as illegible or followed by an asterisk. In the few instances in which Ashenfelter included extra or repeated words, we inserted "[*sic*]" following those words; however, we have not used "[*sic*]" following misspelled words. We have excluded letters, words, and punctuation that Ashenfelter struck out and have transcribed inserted text and superscripts as normal text. Underlined words are reproduced in italics. These same principles apply to Appendixes C and D.

Unless otherwise noted, information in the footnotes comes primarily from works cited in the introduction, Dickinson College catalogs, and genealogical and newspaper databases, including Ancestry.com, genealogybank.com, Fold3.com, and newspapers.com.

Abbreviations

Autobiography   Samuel Whitaker Pennypacker, *The Autobiography of a Penn-sylvanian* (Philadelphia: John C. Winston, 1918)

DCA   Dickinson College Archives and Special Collections, Carlisle, PA

Faculty Minutes   Transcription of the Minutes of the Faculty of Dickinson College, May 17, 1858, to June 25, 1869, Dickinson College Archives and Special Collections, Carlisle, PA

PM   Pennypacker Mills, County of Montgomery, Schwenksville, PA

SMA   Singleton Mercer Ashenfelter

SWP   Samuel Whitaker Pennypacker

VHS   Virginia Museum of History and Culture, Richmond

Key Participants

The following very brief sketches are intended to clarify the identities and relationships of individuals who appear most frequently in the letters. Further biographical information is available in the introduction as well as in a footnote when each person is first mentioned in the correspondence (see the index for the appropriate page numbers).

PHOENIXVILLE

Horace Lloyd, sometimes called "Lloyd" or "Mr. Lord" in the letters, was a member of the Young Men's Literary Union. He later married Mary Eliza "Lide" Vanderslice, who called him "Horry." His younger brother Clement E. Lloyd was also a member of the YMLU.

Samuel W. Pennypacker's cousins Andrew R. Whitaker ("Andy") and Benjamin R. Whitaker ("Ben") were close friends of Ashenfelter's. Other friends included Irvin J. Brower; Richard Denithorne, who went by "Dick"; and Vosburg N. Shaffer, who also attended Dickinson College.

Annie J. Euen was one of Ashenfelter's many love interests. Her father, David Euen, owned a drugstore in Phoenixville and had great disdain for his daughter's suitor. Her mother, Mary Ann Neal, married Euen in 1845.

Singleton's older brother, George Washington Ashenfelter, served in several Union regiments during the Civil War. Their sister Hannah M. Ashenfelter married Isaac Laning in 1865.

DICKINSON COLLEGE

Herman Merrills Johnson was president of Dickinson College during Ashenfelter's time as a student. The faculty at that time included **William C. Wilson**, professor of natural science and chemistry; **William L. Boswell**, professor of German and Greek languages; **John K. Stayman**, professor of Latin, French, philosophy, and English literature; and **Samuel D. Hillman**, professor of mathematics and astronomy. **A. Foster Mullin** was principal of the grammar school when Ashenfelter arrived in 1862.

Ashenfelter's friends at the college included **James Lanius "Giglamps" Himes**, who lived with Shaffer in 4 East College in 1861–62. Ashenfelter wrote frequently of **J. W. Jackson**, whose intellect he found particularly captivating.

During his freshman year, Ashenfelter lived with **Charles W. Bickley** in 9 East College. During his sophomore year, he lived with **James Buchanan Bowman** in 50 West College. During his junior year, he lived with Bowman and Himes in 50 West College. During his senior year, he lived with Himes and **Fairfax Oaks Mills** in 50 West College. He often referred to his roommates as "Chum."

Ashenfelter's romantic interests in Carlisle included **Susan L. Cathcart** (usually called **"Miss Sue"** in the letters) and **Alice Rheem**.

Introduction

ROUGHLY 60 PERCENT OF WHITE MILITARY-AGE MEN IN THE NORTH—some three million people—did not enlist to fight in the Civil War.[1] And yet these Northerners have received remarkably little scholarly attention as a group. Only in the past few decades have historians begun probing the experiences of college students during the war—military-age men who remained at home to receive an education.[2] This dearth of scholarly exploration can be explained, in part, by the paucity of published collections of wartime letters and diaries by students. Within this context, the correspondence that follows—by Dickinson College student Singleton Ashenfelter (1844–1906)—offers a rare and spectacular glimpse into the experiences and intellectual development of one precocious and outgoing, yet contemplative young man who chose to remain at the home front to pursue an education rather than go off to fight in the Civil War.

Singleton Mercer Ashenfelter was born on May 9, 1844, to Henry (1814–91)

1. J. Matthew Gallman, *Defining Duty in the Civil War: Personal Choice, Popular Culture, and the Union Home Front* (Chapel Hill: Univ. of North Carolina Press, 2015), 7–8.

2. See Michael David Cohen, *Reconstructing the Campus: Higher Education and the American Civil War* (Charlottesville: Univ. of Virginia Press, 2012); Julie A. Mujic, "Between Campus and War: Students, Patriotism, and Education at Midwestern Universities during the American Civil War" (PhD diss., Kent State Univ., 2012); Andrew Delbanco, *College: What It Was, Is, and Should Be* (Princeton, NJ: Princeton University Press, 2012); and Roger L. Geiger, *The History of American Higher Education: Learning and Culture from the Founding to World War II* (Princeton, NJ: Princeton Univ. Press, 2014). Older studies include Willis Rudy, *The Campus and a Nation in Crisis: From the American Revolution to Vietnam* (Madison, NJ: Fairleigh Dickinson Univ. Press, 1996); and Ervin L. Jordan Jr., *Charlottesville and the University of Virginia in the Civil War* (Lynchburg, VA: H. E. Howard, 1988).

and Catharine (Kerr) Ashenfelter (1819–99).[3] Henry and Catharine appear to have chosen their son's name in light of a recent local-celebrity murder trial. On February 10, 1843, Singleton "Sink" Mercer of Philadelphia, age twenty-one, shot

Above left: Fig. 1. Singleton M. Ashenfelter. (Courtesy of Pennypacker Mills, County of Montgomery, Schwenksville, PA)

Above right: Fig. 2. Henry Ashenfelter. (Courtesy of Pennypacker Mills, County of Montgomery, Schwenksville, PA)

Left: Fig. 3. Catharine K. Ashenfelter. (Courtesy of Pennypacker Mills, County of Montgomery, Schwenksville, PA)

3. Daniel Kolb Cassel, *A Genealogical History of the Cassel Family in America* (Norristown, PA: Morgan R. Wills, 1896), 412–14.

and killed Mahlon Hutchinson "Hutch" Heberton, age twenty-three. Mercer was livid that Heberton had raped his sixteen-year-old sister, Sarah, at gunpoint and then had boasted about it at local taverns. At his trial Mercer's attorneys claimed that he had committed the homicide while insane. Mercer became something of a local hero for his defense of his family's honor, and when the jury announced an acquittal, crowds cheered his name.[4] As will be clear in the correspondence that follows, Ashenfelter's parents selected an appropriate namesake for their son, who would manage to balance rashness with a commitment to duty and personal honor.

Little is known about Ashenfelter's early years. He grew up in the small, once-prosperous factory town of Phoenixville, Pennsylvania, where his father was a nail manufacturer and manager at the Phoenix Iron Company.[5] By the late 1850s Ashenfelter had developed a close network of friends. His closest friend—and the recipient of the letters reproduced in this book—Samuel W. Pennypacker (1843–1916), later described Ashenfelter as "a little in the rough, but with vital energies and good-hearted."[6]

In Phoenixville Ashenfelter, Pennypacker, and their friends were members of the Young Men's Literary Union (YMLU), which occupied a room above the store of Reeves and Cornett at the corner of Bridge and Main Streets. In addition to a large library of books, the boys subscribed to the daily newspapers from Philadelphia and New York as well as the comic magazine *Punch, The Times* of London, *Harper's Weekly, Vanity Fair,* the London *Art Journal,* and *Scientific Monthly.* Sometimes they had formal debates on topics of the day, and together they cultivated "the arts of composition, declamation and debate." Pennypacker later recalled that these exercises "certainly helped me very much to gain self-possession and to develop the capacity for public speech which I have been called upon to exercise all through life."[7]

As will be seen in Ashenfelter's correspondence, the meetings of the YMLU could become quite heated—even raucous. Years later Pennypacker recalled an incident that occurred between Ashenfelter and their friends Horace Lloyd

4. *Boston Post,* Feb. 16, 1843; *Baltimore Sun,* Apr. 4, 1843; *Ashville (NC) Messenger,* Apr. 21, 1843; *Philadelphia Times,* July 17, 1887.

5. For a brief description of Phoenixville in the Civil War era, see Douglas R. Harper, *"If Thee Must Fight": A Civil War History of Chester County, Pennsylvania* (West Chester: Chester County Historical Society, 1990), 31–35. For an account of Henry Ashenfelter's various careers, see J. Smith Futhey and Gilbert Cope, *History of Chester County, Pennsylvania, with Genealogical and Biographical Sketches* (Philadelphia: Louis H. Everts, 1881), 465–66. The 1850 US census lists him as a "nailor" who owned $1,500 in real estate.

6. *Autobiography,* 68–69.

7. *Autobiography,* 72–73, 101; Horace Lloyd to SWP, Sept. 4, 1864, PM.

Fig. 4. Members of the Young Men's Literary Union (*clockwise from back left*): Horace Lloyd, Richard Deni-thorne, Pennypacker, and Ashenfel-ter. Photograph by M. B. Yarnall of Phoenixville. (Courtesy of the Chester County Historical Society, West Chester, PA)

and Josiah White. "White had force of character," Pennypacker wrote. "Ashenfelter annoyed him, and White emptied a bottle of ink over the light coat of his tormentor. Lloyd occupied two chairs, one with his heels, absorbing the [*New-York*] *Tribune,* which he had held on to during the greater part of the evening. White interrupted this serenity by setting fire to the paper." During the war, local women and girls used the rooms of the YMLU to make uniforms and other supplies for soldiers.[8]

When the war came, White became a lieutenant in the 1st Pennsylvania Reserves (also known as the 30th Pennsylvania Infantry). He was wounded at Antietam on September 17, 1862, and again at the Battle of the Wilderness in May 1864, from which he died at a hospital in Washington, DC. After White's death

---

8. *Autobiography,* 72–73, 89–90. During the war, Singleton's mother, Catharine, and sister, Hannah (1842–1907), were both involved with the Ladies' Aid Society of Phoenixville. See SWP, *Annals of Phoenixville and Its Vicinity: From the Settlement to the Year 1871* (Philadelphia: Bavis and Pennypacker, 1872), 230.

Fig. 5. Josiah White. (Courtesy of Pennypacker Mills, County of Montgomery,
Schwenksville, PA)

Pennypacker assumed the presidency of the YMLU. From Dickinson, Ashenfelter wrote of wanting to visit "Whitey's grave." Pennypacker recollected years
later that when White's "body was brought to Phoenixville, from the Wilderness
battlefield, where he was killed, in accordance with a custom which still lingered
[at the time of the war], Lloyd, Ashenfelter and I watched over it all night, and
we carried him to his grave in the Dunker graveyard, at the Green Tree."[9]

In 1862 Ashenfelter left his friends behind and moved to Carlisle, where he
enrolled at Dickinson College. Chartered in 1783, Dickinson was established to
instill "virtuous principles and liberal knowledge . . . into the minds of the rising
generation" through instruction in the "useful arts, sciences and literature."[10]
As with so many institutions, Dickinson suffered a drastic decline in enrollment at the start of the Civil War and consequently faced serious financial bur-
dens. In December 1863 college president Herman Merrills Johnson petitioned
Simon Cameron—one of the wealthiest, most powerful, and most corrupt
politicians and businessmen of the nineteenth century—to create an endowed

9. *Autobiography,* 73, 89.
10. *An Act for the establishment of a college at the borough of Carlisle, in the county of Cum-
berland, in the state of Pennsylvania,* Sept. 9, 1783, in *Laws of the Commonwealth of Pennsylvania,* 4 vols. (Philadelphia: John Bioren, 1810), 2:71–72.

Fig. 6. West College, ca. 1861–74. The oldest building on campus, it contained student living spaces and classrooms during the nineteenth century. The cornerstone was laid in 1803, and classes began to meet in the building in 1805, although construction was not completed until 1821. Today "Old West" houses administrative offices. (Courtesy of the Library of Congress)

Fig. 7. East College, ca. 1870. Built in 1836, it included recitation rooms and housing for students. The college president lived in the eastern end of the building until 1890. During the Gettysburg Campaign of 1863, East College served as a Confederate hospital. Today several humanities departments occupy the building. (Courtesy of the Library of Congress)

Fig. 8. Pres. Herman Mer-
rills Johnson. (Courtesy
of Archives and Special
Collections, Dickinson
College, Carlisle, PA)

professorship to help return the school to financial stability. In his letter Johnson boasted of the benefits and virtues of the institution and lamented the
challenges that war had brought. "We have suffered severely by the rebellion,"
he wrote, having "lost about half our students at a stroke." Moreover, the college's endowment fund was collected largely in Virginia and Maryland and was
held primarily by a corporate board in Baltimore, several of whose members
"proved to be secessionists—*traitors*—& made every exertion to deprive us of
our funds, purely on political grounds." Johnson stressed the importance of a
liberal-arts education and that Dickinson alumni were "*worthy* the regard of
the *patriot*." He urged Cameron that, "with the proper endowment, Dickinson
would become at once for Pennsylvania, what Harvard is for Massachusetts &
Yale for Connecticut."[11]

11. Herman M. Johnson to Simon Cameron, Dec. 15, 1863, Simon Cameron Papers, Dau-
phin County Historical Society, Harrisburg, PA; James Henry Morgan, *Dickinson College:
The History of One Hundred and Fifty Years, 1783–1933* (Carlisle, PA: Dickinson College,
1933), 312–13, 318–26; H. Calista McCabe, "Rev. Herman M. Johnson, D.D.," *Ladies' Reposi-
tory* (May 1875), 454–56; Collections Register, Herman Merrills Johnson Papers, MC 2003.9,
DCA; John R. Thelin, *A History of American Higher Education,* 2nd ed. (Baltimore: Johns
Hopkins Univ. Press, 2011), 74–75.

Although located in Pennsylvania, Dickinson had many students from the South. In fact, in 1860, 49 of the school's 116 students hailed from slave states. Nevertheless, even as war broke out, the student body maintained a high level of collegiality. As students left to enlist or made clear their allegiances, Dickinson was fairly untouched by the hostile divisions that plagued other campuses. Just one week after the surrender of Fort Sumter in April 1861, one student from Maryland wrote to a Northern peer: "Though I am a secessionist, yet I am your friend. May prosperity attend you in all you do, except in making war upon the South." Another student joked, "If I wear the 'Phi Kap' badge, don't shoot me, Frank."[12]

College life in the nineteenth century could be rowdy. Students participated in practical jokes (some of which are described in Ashenfelter's letters), snowball fights, dangerous physical activities, and other sports.[13] Sometimes pranks could lead to dire consequences for the students—including expulsion.

On February 2, 1856, William T. Kinzer, a Dickinson student from Virginia, wrote in his diary: "Great times! A college rebellion! Three or four of the students have been expelled for putting tar on the black boards. The students have a paper in circulation stating that they will not attend recitations unless the students who have been expelled are reinstated. Notices have been posted up that there will be a speaking on the steps of W.C. [West College] at 6 oclock." A large body of students gathered to hear the speeches, but by 8 P.M., Kinzer observed, nothing had happened: "A Humbug, no speaking. They had better be in their rooms studying. A number of students have been standing on the steps of E.C. [East College] and there is a good deal of excitement. I think it will pass off without any harm." The next day proved more eventful, according to Kinzer: "College rebellion is going

Historian Michael David Cohen contends that colleges "refashioned themselves as vehicles of war" and "harnessed" themselves "to serve wartime needs." Dickinson College was financially unable to do what Cohen describes, and Julie Mujic has found that the experience of midwestern colleges was more similar to Dickinson. See Julie Mujic, "Save a School to Save a Nation: Faculty Responses to the Civil War at Midwestern Universities," in *So Conceived and So Dedicated: Intellectual Life in the Civil War–Era North*, ed. Lorien Foote and Kanisorn Wongsrichanalai (New York: Fordham Univ. Press, 2015), 110–28.

12. Morgan, *Dickinson College*, 312; Bell Irvin Wiley, "Johnny Reb and Billy Yank," in *Early Dickinsoniana: The Boyd Lee Spahr Lectures in Americana, 1957–1961* (Carlisle, PA: Library of Dickinson College, 1961), 141. By contrast, students at Princeton University had at least one violent outburst when Northern students held a Southern-sympathizing student under a water pump in September 1861.

13. See, for example, Mujic, "Between Campus and War," 190–92; William T. Kinzer Diary, Feb. 4–5, Apr. 13, 1857, VHS; William Samuel Grantham to brother, Apr. 22, 1854, Larue Family Papers, sec. 4, VHS; and Charles Coleman Sellers, *Dickinson College: A History* (Middleton, CT: Wesleyan Univ., 1973), 242–44.

on yet. About one hundred students have signed the paper of yesterday. The faculty say that they will not give way. The excitement is very high. I hope it will pass off without any harm. I heard that the president said the college is in a critical condition." On February 4 the "rebellion is going on yet. Neither party will give in. I cannot tell how it will end." But after another day, things seemed to be nearing an "amicable agreement." Throughout the fifth Kinzer updated his diary. At 10 A.M. a faculty member told the students that they were in the wrong. At noon things were "at a stand still." At 3 P.M., though, he noted that the "students are giving way." Two hours later the students attended evening prayers so that "peace is restored." By 7 P.M. Kinzer could gladly report, "The insurrection is over." But the next morning he was in for a surprise. "The seats, benches, tables, and black boards of the Grammar School are tar[r]ed," he wrote in his diary. "That is all."[14]

Not all students wanted to participate in such disruptions to their studies. In October 1861 James Lanius Himes—whom Ashenfelter would affectionately call "Giglamps" and who would become his closest friend during his freshman year at Dickinson—observed, "I find that College boys are a pretty bad set of fellows, a great many of them drink, play cards & run out after profligate women &c. but I have resolved to keep out of all such things." Himes preferred to work hard in his classes and to spend his leisure time reading. "The boys here call me 'Old Grimes, that good old man,'" he wrote his brother. But even he did not like to feel as though he was being monitored too closely by the faculty. One night Dr. Johnson visited Himes's room to see how he was settling into college life. Himes told the college president that his roommate "was out calling on some ladies," after which Johnson "talked to me about joining the church, tending class &c." for about fifteen minutes. Eventually Johnson said "good evening" and left the room. Himes "bowed him out with a 'call again Dr.' which among the college boys means 'stay away as long as you please.'"[15]

Himes's "chum," or roommate, Vosburg Shaffer, was an old friend of Ashenfelter's from Phoenixville. But Himes did not care for his personal habits and wished he was "a little more studious." Shaffer was "a poor scholar" and "a little wilder, than I would have wished, but otherwise he is as nice a fellow as I could want," according to Himes. "Chum & I get along pretty well but he is not the kind of a fellow I would like," he continued. "Chum goes out to see the ladies about twice a week, he has been coaxing me to go along, saying that he has a standing invitation to bring his chum along but I told him I would not have any thing to do with

14. Kinzer Diary, Feb. 2–6, 1856, VHS; Sellers, *Dickinson College*, 244.
15. Himes to brother, Oct. 10, 1861, Himes Papers, DCA.

Fig. 9. Dickinson College students in 1863. As listed on the reverse, they are: [Benjamin Peffer] Lamberton, [Henry Clay] Speak, [S. Townsend] Armstrong, [James Buchanan] Bowman, Wilson, and [James Lanius] Himes. Photograph by C. L. Lochman of Carlisle. (Courtesy of Archives and Special Collections, Dickinson College, Carlisle, PA)

the girls for a while to come yet." Himes particularly did not like that Shaffer used tradesmen's "slang" and "swears a little more than I like but I cant stop him."[16]

Even studious students like Himes had difficulty focusing on schoolwork when spring rolled around. "We are having delightful weather just now," he wrote in May 1862, "& numerous groups of students can be seen throughout the campus, enjoying the shade of some green tree. The campus is beginning to look beautiful; the grass appears to be one immense sheet of green downy velvet; the trees are commencing to leaf & the birds are already heard to warble their enchanting melodies." How ironic, to him, that the end of the semester was "when we have to study the hardest & when the weather makes one feel more like lieing under a shade tree talking, than being confined to your room studying."[17]

Unlike Himes, Ashenfelter cared little for studying and participated in his fair share of hijinks. Writing in 1867, Ashenfelter mused about how he had "always shirked" his studies: "At college I rested satisfied with personal popularity,

16. Himes to brother, Oct. 10, 17, 1861, Himes Papers, DCA.
17. Himes to brother, May 3, 1862, Himes Papers, DCA.

& the reputation of being 'a thunderin' smart fellah.'"[18] Like Himes, however, he resented Dr. Johnson's tightfisted control over the college. After dark Johnson "will track a student all over town, creeping along like a snake, watching, and coming up when least expected. It is no unusual thing for him to go down town, walk into a billiard saloon, and scatter the players with, 'to your rooms gentlemen, to your rooms'; and frequently, at midnight, in slippers, he sneaks over College, making sure that every student is in his room, and that no mischief is plotting."[19] But the faculty were generally powerless to stop college students from pulling pranks. "The boys here are always on the alert to play tricks on the Proffessors," wrote Himes in 1861. And they found opportunities to defy Dr. Johnson too. In 1860, when several students wore the badges of fraternities and secret societies, including Phi Kappa Sigma, to their recitations, Johnson threatened to expel them. But the next day found the entire student body wearing various badges, "and they have been wearing them ever since."[20]

Over time Ashenfelter gave up his childish ways—including drinking alcohol and lying—and devoted himself to reading and intellectual development (although, amazingly, he considered himself "devilish lazy"). He borrowed books from the library and participated in the school's literary societies, including the Belles Lettres Literary Society and Union Philosophical Society, both of which had been founded in the eighteenth century.[21] (Ashenfelter joined the Union Philosophical Society as well as the Phi Kappa Sigma fraternity.) His letters trace his intellectual development during this time (including discussion of the books and poetry he read, a rare find in Civil War correspondence[22]), his relationships

---

18. SMA to SWP, June 12, 1867, PM.

19. Letter of Apr. 25, 1862. For another instance of Johnson chasing down pranksters, see William Samuel Grantham to brother, Apr. 22, 1854, Larue Family Papers, sec. 4, VHS.

20. Himes to brother, Oct. 10, 27, 1861, Himes Papers, DCA.

21. Charles F. Himes, *A Sketch of Dickinson College, Carlisle, Penn'a* (Harrisburg, PA: Lane S. Hart, 1879), 83–86. Famous members of the Belles Lettres Literary Society included Roger Brooke Taney, class of 1795, who went on to become chief justice of the United States. On the importance of literary societies to a young man's education and maturation, see Timothy J. Williams, *Intellectual Manhood: University, Self, and Society in the Antebellum South* (Chapel Hill: Univ. of North Carolina Press, 2015), 38–42, 173–98.

22. During the war, Americans wrote far less in depth about what they were reading than they had previously. See Ronald J. Zboray and Mary Saracino Zboray, "Cannonballs and Books: Reading and the Disruption of Social Ties on the New England Home Front," in *The War Was You and Me: Civilians in the American Civil War*, ed. Joan E. Cashin (Princeton, NJ: Princeton Univ. Press, 2002), 245. For a helpful analysis of the reading culture of young white Southerners in this era, see Timothy J. Williams, "The Readers' South: Literature, Region, and Identity in the Civil War Era," *Journal of the Civil War Era* 8 (Dec. 2018): 564–90.

with friends at home, his aspirations for postcollegiate life, and his struggles with depression as he grew into adulthood. In short, they offer a rich, introspective view into the experiences of a middle-class Northern white youth who experienced life on the home front during a period of incredible social transformation in the United States.[23]

Ashenfelter's letters reflect what historian Timothy J. Williams calls "intellectual manhood." According to Williams, intellectual manhood involves "knowing one's self, controlling one's mind, acting wisely, and speaking intelligently." This concept was central to an antebellum undergraduate education. The structure, pedagogy, and curriculum of nineteenth-century American universities were geared toward helping students "transition from boyhood to manhood"—to learn to restrain immature impulses, to be sober minded and mentally disciplined, to be industrious, and to be able to function as independent adults. In his study of the University of North Carolina in the years before the Civil War, Williams observes that this process of maturation was the "most pressing concern" for college students. "Not quite boys and not yet men, collegians were youths. Their experiences at college, as well as the way they viewed their education, were defined by a constant tug of war between boyhood and manhood," he writes. "These tensions were perfectly ordinary developmental struggles of upper- and middle-class southern whites; sometimes they hindered education but often times they opened up creative opportunities for young men to fashion adult selves." In a related way, Williams finds that college students' "pervasive focus on maturation made the individual self the primary focus among students. Questions of how the self was defined, composed, articulated, and empowered therefore framed not only young men's maturation but also the content and exercises of university life and learning."[24] No concept could better capture Ashenfelter's experiences as an undergraduate at Dickinson College as he transitioned from being a suburban boy to a college-educated man.

The letters reveal a great deal about one young man's personal philosophy and religious views. During his time at Dickinson, Ashenfelter grew increasingly cynical about religion. His letters to Pennypacker in early 1863 intimate

23. On the difficulties facing young men and women as they entered adulthood during the tumultuous mid-nineteenth century, see Jon Grinspan, "A Birthday Like None Other: Turning Twenty-One in the Age of Popular Politics," in *Age in America: The Colonial Era to the Present*, ed. Corinne T. Field and Nicholas L. Syrett (New York: New York Univ. Press, 2015), 86–93.

24. Williams, *Intellectual Manhood*, 2, 6, 18, 21–22, 31, 35, 51, 93, 97–98. On the ways that antebellum New England colleges prepared young men for adulthood, see Kanisorn Wongsrichanalai, *Northern Character: College-Educated New Englanders, Honor, Nationalism, and Leadership in the Civil War Era* (New York: Fordham Univ. Press, 2016), 19–34.

his doubts about Christianity, and while he believed in "a creator & governor of the universe," he attributed all formal religion to "the worn out records of a superstitious age." Doubt turned to contempt, and in the coming months he began to feel "utterly disgusted at the superstition which supports so blind a beliefe." By 1864 Ashenfelter "believed in a God no longer" and called himself "an utter skeptic in all things."[25] This skepticism also often infused his relationships with other people as well as his view of himself. "I am disgusted with humanity," he admitted, "& myself as a part of it." He frequently called himself a "fool" and harped on the general selfishness and egotism of mankind. Occasionally, his dark view of humanity affected him deeply, and Ashenfelter wrote about being "terribly blue." He once told Pennypacker: "I am disgusted with everything. I can do nothing but sit & think of the *dark* phazes of human existence. At such moments, my feelings approximate those of the suicide."[26]

Ashenfelter's voice and personality emerge forcefully in his letters. He was arrogant, erudite, witty, impulsive, ambitious, self-interested, introspective, and deeply intellectual. As might be expected, much of his attention was on romance. Yet even in this arena, he wrote, "love & every other emotion must acknowledge itself inferior to the will which is inspired by ambition." This principle was borne out in his relationships with women. When discussing his romantic feelings for Annie Euen—a young, respectable girl back in Phoenixville—he told Pennypacker that he would marry only for wealth, political influence, and "the promotion of my ends." Ironically, he faulted other women for being as "supremely selfish" as he was. Ashenfelter found one Carlisle girl, Alice Rheem, to be "just such a woman as would sacrifice all tender feeling, whenever & wherever it stood between . . . her & what she considered her advantage." When he tried to end their relationship, Ashenfelter found it rather difficult "to get myself out of the scrape with apparent honor." At first he told Rheem that his future was too uncertain to continue their relationship, but she assured him that his prospects were as bright as any. To prove his incompetence, Ashenfelter purposefully performed so horribly in an oratorical contest at Dickinson that a professor remonstrated, "Why, Ashenfelter you hav'nt done yourself justice." To this he replied, "I know it," then added, "but I've done what I wished to do."[27]

Ashenfelter did little to conceal his cynicism. Indeed, his letters reveal a frankness not only with Pennypacker but with others as well. When Annie Euen

25. Letters of Mar. 8, May 30, Nov. 22, 1863, and Mar. 19, 1864.

26. Letter of Mar. 19, 1864. On the pervasiveness of these dark and depressive characteristics of young people's private writings, see Grinspan, "Birthday Like None Other."

27. Letters of Nov. 22, 1863, Mar. 19, 1864, and Feb. [n.d.], 1865. This speech, entitled "Capital Punishment," is reproduced in Appendix D.

asked if he had recently been drinking, he initially lied by omission but later admitted that he had.[28] He also refused to attend church, not simply because he was an atheist but because "by an attendance at church, I tacitly or at least apparently admit the truth of what is there advanced." His refusal to even implicitly support what he, in fact, opposed did not end at religion. Ashenfelter vehemently disapproved of the union between his friend Horace Lloyd and Mary Eliza "Lide" Vanderslice. He remained baffled at what Lloyd saw in her homely appearance. "I do not see how he can love her," he wrote Pennypacker, "& as far as *sensual* enjoyment is concerned, a man of sense would look elsewhere." Evidently, he made no effort to conceal such thoughts to Lloyd and continually sought to convince him of his foolishness, supplying the "occasional assurance that he is a darned fool. If he marries her, I'll make it d—d fool." Lloyd shrugged off his friend's warnings and married Lide anyway. Even after the wedding, Ashenfelter ostentatiously refused to offer his congratulations.[29]

Perhaps most importantly, these letters reveal a great deal about male friendship among middle-class Northerners in the mid-nineteenth century. Throughout his time at Dickinson College, Pennypacker remained Ashenfelter's closest friend and confidant. When lamenting the shallowness of his college friendships, he told Pennypacker, "I almost imagine, I will go mad, if I cannot have some one, between whome, & myself, a mutual interchange of thought, will not be a mutual bore." As time went on, he confessed that he was "not homesick, but friendsick." Although the two often disagreed on intellectual and religious matters, Ashenfelter greatly valued Pennypacker's opinions and frequently asked for his views on various subjects. Their discussions on religion, politics, romance, and their futures reveal an intimacy missing in Ashenfelter's other friendships at Dickinson. Indeed, he withheld nothing from Pennypacker. "I could open up to you the most secret chambers of my heart," he declared. "In short you are the only person living, who, with my consent, may know Sing Ashenfelter as well as I do."[30]

Pennypacker's letters became an important source of encouragement for his friend at Dickinson. Ashenfelter took to drinking some months into his college career. When he first arrived, he boasted that while his classmates went out to

28. Years later he admitted: "Annie doubted me because some of my lies she had detected. It would have been strange if she hadn't—the number I told her." See SMA to SWP, Aug. 5, 1868, PM.

29. Letters of Mar. 19, 1864, and Jan. 5, 1865.

30. Letters of Nov. 22, 1863, and Mar. 19, May [n.d.], 1864. The intimacy in SMA's correspondence reflects much of what is described in E. Anthony Rotundo, "Romantic Friendship: Male Intimacy and Middle-Class Youth in the Northern United States, 1800–1900," *Journal of Social History* 23 (Autumn 1989): 1–25.

drink, he maintained the "moral courage to refrain." Eventually, however, "some mad impulse which urged me on to tempt all of [the] evil in my nature" got the better of him and led to some embarrassing incidents, including one that brought him into ill repute with Annie Euen. His drinking problem became a continual source of self-loathing. Finally, Pennypacker appears to have told him, "if friendship can add ought to the appeals of love, then *I conjure* you to stop now." This admonition seems to have worked. "What was impossible to *love*"—meaning what Annie could not bring about in him—"*friendship* has accomplished." Ashenfelter never drank again while at college.[31]

Surprisingly, the war only rarely appears in these letters—revealing how a Northern college student buried in studies could live in an environment insulated from an event that was consuming the lives of so many other young men.[32] This lack of focus on the war underscores a little-appreciated point once made by historian J. Matthew Gallman, that "much of Northern society carried on seemingly untouched by the conflict."[33] Ashenfelter occasionally commented on politics, which he saw as a "humbug." Although a Republican, he criticized the leaders of both political parties alike. He vigorously opposed universal suffrage and opined on federal Reconstruction policy. Still, he told Pennypacker that he was—and always had been—a "pro-war abolitionist" and believed that "the South should be made to understand that she cannot do just as she pleases."[34]

Ashenfelter did have one brief encounter with military service. During Confederate general Robert E. Lee's invasion of Maryland in September 1862, several Dickinson students joined a militia company to help stop the rebels from advancing into Pennsylvania. Ashenfelter found himself swept up in the frenzied excitement in Carlisle. Having "caught the prevalent feeling," he left Dickinson, joined the "milishe," and boarded a train "amid a profusion of cheers and tears."

31. Letters of Mar. 4, 1863, and July 25, 1864. SWP's mother worried about the influence SMA had on her son. "Have you learned to smoke yet?" she asked him. "Sing is such a smoker I expect to hear, soon, that you are smoking too—You had better not begin, it is much easier to learn a bad habit, than to leave it after." See A. M. W. Pennypacker to SWP, [n.d.], 1863, PM.

32. SMA's experience is in keeping with that of other college students at the time. At Yale in 1864 the freshman class held a debate on the wisdom of Lincoln's reconstruction policy. One student complained to a Democratic member of Congress, "A student has not the opportunity of watching the politics of the day as our duties here keep us employed fully." See Casper S. Bigler to Charles R. Buckalew, Apr. 6, May 24, 1864, Charles R. Buckalew Papers, Manuscript Division, Library of Congress, Washington, DC.

33. J. Matthew Gallman, *The North Fights the Civil War: The Home Front* (Chicago: Ivan R. Dee, 1994), 83–84.

34. Letters of Aug. 5, 1864, and June 6, 1865.

Fig. 10. Gov. Andrew G. Curtin, class of
1837. (Courtesy of Jonathan W. White)

His time bearing arms would be short lived, however, and he never saw action.
Dickinson's president wrote to Pennsylvania governor Andrew G. Curtin argu-
ing that the governor would "better serve the Commonwealth" by releasing the
boys than by prolonging their service. Doing so, Johnson said, would be "pro-
tecting the College in this crisis." Curtin, a Dickinson alumnus (class of 1837),
ordered the dozen or so students to be discharged from their military service.
Ashenfelter subsequently described his brief enlistment in a terse, comical letter
to Pennypacker.[35]

Ashenfelter left no record of the Confederate invasion of Pennsylvania during the summer of 1863. Unfortunately, he also chose not to attend the cemetery dedication at Gettysburg later that year. In order to supply an account of
Dickinson College during the Gettysburg Campaign, Appendix C includes a
firsthand account by an alumnus who was living in Carlisle at the time.

Following Ashenfelter's graduation from Dickinson in 1865, he moved to

35. Letter of Sept. 28, 1862; Herman M. Johnson to Andrew G. Curtin, Sept. 15, 1862,
DCA; Morgan, *Dickinson College*, 313–14.

Philadelphia and lived with Pennypacker in a rented room at 520 Spruce Street. "It was modest enough, but kept bright and cleanly, and the impression even today is one of luxurious enjoyment," recalled Pennypacker many years later. Both men studied law under Peter McCall, a prominent Democratic lawyer and former Philadelphia mayor. McCall appears to have been pleased with Pennypacker for bringing Ashenfelter to his attention, for he wrote in August 1865, "I shall be very glad to make the acquaintance of your friend whom you have initiated in the office, quite to my satisfaction."[36]

Pennypacker would go on to have a successful career in politics and law, eventually becoming a judge on Philadelphia's court of common pleas (1889–1902) and then the twenty-third governor of Pennsylvania (1903–7). Ashenfelter, by contrast, seemed more restless. For a brief period he edited the *National Standard* in Salem, New Jersey. At first he found himself "comfortably situated" there and "rapidly" making friends, but he soon became disgusted with politics. "I don't care a curse for the Radical or Conservative side of these political questions," he wrote to Pennypacker in September 1866. "All my enthusiasm is forced."[37] He also hated the newspaper business. "Type setting threw me into horrors perpetual," he confessed, "& with editorship I became so disgusted in five months, that I wanted to ship before the mast on a merchant vessel."[38]

In late 1866 Ashenfelter departed on a sea voyage around Cape Horn, landing in Valparaiso, Chile, in March 1867. He spent nearly two years on the west coast of South America and, for a period, served as a consular clerk in Ecuador. In one of his first letters back to Pennypacker, he remarked: "I have no intention to enter into a lengthy description of the various matters of interest that have come under my observation since the barque reached this port, but will sum up the result of my experience, by simply remarking that your friend is an ass. I always was you know." Years later in his autobiography, Pennypacker briefly recalled his friend's adventures: "When Ashenfelter returned from an abode of sixteen months in Guayaquil, where he became secretary to the United States Consul, had the yellow fever, smuggled cocoa and secured, together with a profit of $1,500, a knife cut across the chin and a bullet wound in the leg, I began to study Spanish and to use it in conversation with him."[39]

---

36. *Autobiography*, 112; Peter McCall to SWP, Aug. 25, 1865, PM. McCall's papers are held in the Cadwalader Collection at the Historical Society of Pennsylvania, Philadelphia.

37. SMA to SWP, Sept. 23, 1866, PM.

38. SMA to SWP, Sept. 23, 1866, June 12, 1867, PM. SMA did not end up shipping on a merchant vessel but instead on a bark heading for South America.

39. SMA to SWP, June 12, 1867, PM; *Autobiography*, 145.

Ashenfelter returned to the United States in 1868, completed his legal train-
ing, and practiced law in Rock Island, Illinois, where he also served as an editor
of the *Daily Union*. He never lost his irreverent approach to life. In a political
speech one night in Rock Island, Ashenfelter told the crowd "that it was no[t] &
never had been the aim of the Republican Party to perpetuate sexual—sexual—
sectional animosities." He gleefully informed Pennypacker, "Some of the women
snickered, hang them!"[40]

In 1870 Ashenfelter traveled to New Mexico Territory, where he was appointed
US attorney by Pres. Ulysses S. Grant.[41] He remained in the West for the rest of
his life, practicing law and editing newspapers in various cities, including Silver
City, New Mexico, and Colorado Springs. In New Mexico he fell in love with a
young woman named Jennett Bennett, who went by Nettie. "Nettie is a good
girl and comes of good surroundings," he wrote to Pennypacker. "In music she
is brilliant and, I think I may say, talented. Her face and form are decidedly attractive, her health excellent, and her manner impressive. She writes and talks
readily and well, and altogether reflects credit on my taste."[42] The couple married
on November 21, 1872, and went on to have five children, one of whom died in
infancy. (Ashenfelter's romantic exploits from 1865 until he met and married Nettie are described in greater detail in the epilogue.) But he and Pennypacker never
relinquished their friendship. (In fact, they became family when Pennypacker
married Ashenfelter's cousin, Virginia Broomall, on October 20, 1870.) When, in
the early 1890s, Ashenfelter appealed a case to the US Supreme Court, he retained
his old friend as his lawyer. Judge Ashenfelter, as he was known by the end of his
life, died suddenly of heart failure on the morning of January 23, 1906.[43]

Over the years Ashenfelter sent Pennypacker some three hundred letters, de-
tailing his college life, his travels in South America, his service as US attorney in
New Mexico Territory, and the other events of his life in the West. These letters
remain with Pennypacker's personal papers at Pennypacker Mills in Schwenksville, Pennsylvania. They are a remarkable record of a friendship that lasted for
more than half a century.

40. SMA to SWP, Oct. 26, 1868, PM.

41. SWP traveled to Washington, DC, twice in 1870 to petition for SMA's appointment.
See SWP to Sarah A. Whitaker, Nov. 1, 1870, PM.

42. SMA to SWP, Oct. 31, 1872, PM.

43. Cassel, *Genealogical History*, 412–14; SMA to W. F. Pleasants, Nov. 18, 1870, Record
Group 60 (General Records of the Department of Justice), Entry 9-A (Letters Received by
the Attorney General, 1809–1870), National Archives at College Park, MD; SMA to Andrew
Johnson, Aug. 24, 1866, Andrew Johnson Papers, Manuscript Division, Library of Congress,
Washington, DC; *Ashenfelter v. Territory of New Mexico ex rel. Wade*, 154 US 493 (1893); *Den-
ver Post*, Jan. 23, 1906. SMA's official correspondence as US attorney is held in RG 60, Entry
56 (Source-Chronological File, 1870–1884), National Archives at College Park.

CHAPTER ONE

1862

Dickinson College, Apr. 25th 1862.

Dear Pennie,

Just four weeks ago this very day, and at about this hour, (7 A.M.) I bade you farewell at Phoenix depot and now after this interval of silence, I sit down to write to you. As I have been rather derelict, I will offer you a batch of excuses. First, I have been so devilish lazy since I have been here that I could scarcely find time to write to my relatives, *female acquaintances,* and to Mr. Llord;[1] whose connection with me, as shown in the trivett*, gives him the preference. Second, I wished to "learn the ropes"; to become acquainted with the ins and outs of College life before I addressed you, in order that I might have material enough to make an interesting letter. Third,—but enough of this; I suppose two will excuse my slowness.

Previous to giving you my experience of College, I will describe the Faculty. The Pres. is Herman M. Johnson, *D.D.*[2] I do not think I was ever so much disappointed in the looks of a man before. He is as short, lean, dried up, and sneaking looking personage as ever I set my eyes on. Nor does his character give the lie to his face; for after dark he will track a student all over town, creeping along like a snake, watching, and coming up when least expected. It is no unusual thing for

1. "Mr. Lord" was a nickname for Horace Lloyd (1839–1911), a member of the Young Men's Literary Union, whom SWP described in his autobiography as "an upright, narrow and methodical clerk in the [Phoenixville] bank." The similarity between "Lord" and "Lloyd" may explain why SMA spelled it "Llord" here.

2. Herman Merrills Johnson (1815–68) served as professor of English literature for ten years before his election in 1860 as Dickinson's twelfth president.

him to go down town, walk into a billiard saloon, and scatter the players with, "to your rooms gentlemen, to your rooms"; and frequently, at midnight, in slippers, he sneaks over College, making sure that every student is in his room, and that no mischief is plotting. So much for him.

The other members of the faculty are Wm. C. Wilson,[3] A.M., professor of natural science &c, Rev. Wm. L. Boswell,[4] A.M. professor of Greek & German, John K. Stayman,[5] professor of Latin & French, Saml. D. Hillman[6] A.M. professor of mathematics and A. F. Mullen,[7] principal of Grammar schools; these are all perfect gentlemen, and each looks as if he understood his own department, and they do.

3. William C. Wilson (1827–65) graduated from Dickinson College in 1850 and in 1854 was elected a professor of natural science and chemistry. As will be described in chapter 4, he died tragically and suddenly shortly before SMA graduated in 1865. Wilson appears to have built a wonderful rapport with most of his students. Once, when students in one class pulled a prank on him by leaving a calf at his desk in his recitation room, Wilson quipped, "Your class is large enough already." But others were underwhelmed by him. William T. Kinzer, a student from Virginia, wrote in his diary in 1857: "Recited in Anatomy to Prof. Wilson. Asked him a question about the mince pie, which he either could or did not answer." The next day: "Heard Prof. Wilson lecture at 4 P.M. Not great. Not much. Little." William T. Kinzer Diary, Mar. 9–10, 1857, VHS.

4. William L. Boswell (1828–1912) graduated from Dickinson in 1848 and returned to the college to teach math from 1857 to 1860, when he became a professor of German and Greek languages. In 1881 he joined the college's board of trustees. According to SMA's friend and classmate James Lanius Himes, "none of the boys like him, he looks as savage as a bear." Yet Himes quickly came to appreciate Boswell. "I begin to like Proff. Boswell very much, he explains a great deal & very readily answers the questions put to him." Himes to brother, Oct. 10, Nov. 17, 1861, Himes Papers, DCA.

5. John K. Stayman (1823–82) graduated from Dickinson in 1841 and went on to teach Latin, French, philosophy, and English literature. According to some accounts, he was a pushover with the students and would shorten assignments if they complained. In 1874 Stayman, Prof. Samuel D. Hillman, and Prof. William Trickett (1840–1928) were accused of "misconduct and breaches of the laws of the college" after cooperating with a group of disorderly students. The three were subsequently removed from the Dickinson faculty. The board's decision garnered local controversy, as it seemed to stem more from personal than professional reasons.

6. Samuel Dickinson Hillman (1825–1912) was a professor of mathematics and astronomy at Dickinson College from 1860 until his removal in 1874. He was known for being "keen and merry . . . and the best chess-player in a faculty of chess-players." In 1868 he temporarily served as president of the college immediately following the death of Herman M. Johnson.

7. A. Foster Mullin (1837–1916), class of 1858, held various leadership roles in the college's alumni association and also served as principal of the Dickinson grammar school until 1862, when Henry C. Cheston replaced him.

A few nights after I came here an attempt was made to squib me; the squib-bers tied my door shut, and then put[t]ing in the quills commenced to pound on the door. [F]ortunately for my rest, the powder did not go off; when they do explode they fill the room with such intollerable stench that sleep for the remainder of the night is impossible.[8] They kept up the pounding at my door from 11½ until about midnight, when having aroused the College, and there be-ing a probability of Doc. Johnson's appearance, they thought it prudent to beat a retreat. They did not make much for neither chum nor I got out of bed. A few nights afterwards I joined a party of squibbers myself. A new fellow came on from Baltimore,[9] and Shaffer,[10] four other fellows, and myself resolved to initiate him. Accordingly squibs being prepared, (by filling quills with alternate layers of dry and wet powder) and having ropes we set to work. Tied the door, sent the squibs flying through the key hole, and commenced to pound the door with clubs. When we had kept this nuisance up for about ten minutes, and stop[p]ed to take a little rest, one of our number, a fellow named Bowman,[11] was seized by the arm by a Prof. who had stolen upon us unawares. (It was near midnight, and very dark[.]) Bowman, with a sudden jerk, landed the Prof. on the floor, and we all run out of the hall, and closing the door after us held it so that he could not get out except by a round-about way. He came and tried the door, but finding it fast, started back for the other way, while we 'cut stick' for our rooms. If a profes-sor had called five minutes after he would have found us all in bed.

All students are required to be in their rooms during study hours. The Profs. make visits at irregular times in order to see that they *are* in. The night before last I was sitting in the room of a young fellow named Burnight,[12] enjoying a

8. Squibbing was a popular form of prank at Dickinson at the time. Another student de-scribed squibbing two classmates a few years earlier. See Kinzer Diary, Apr. 13, 1857, VHS.

9. Dickinson had several students from Baltimore during the war years. This one may have been E. P. Long, who was the only Baltimorean in SMA's class that year.

10. Vosburg N. Shaffer (1842–1926) of Chester County was the son of the overseer of the Phoenix Iron Company. As a freshman he roomed with James Lanius Himes (see note 35, p. 28, and the introduction), who said he "suppose[d] he is of a very respectable family." During the Gettysburg Campaign, Shaffer served as a corporal in the 34th Pennsylvania Volunteer Militia from June 29 to August 10, 1863. Following the war, Shaffer became the editor and publisher of the *Phoenixville Independent* and the *Daily Independent*. He also became a Freemason.

11. James Buchanan Bowman of Carlisle graduated in 1865 and became a bookkeeper.

12. Wilbur Hyland Burnite (1845–1918) of Felton, Delaware, was a member of the class of 1866 but never graduated from Dickinson College. He was elected to the state legislature in 1876, became a director of the State Agricultural Society in 1887, and served as the state trea-surer from 1891 to 1895. See David Clark Burnite V, *The Burnite Genealogy and Family History* (N.p., 1982), 44, 66–70.

game of whist during study hours, when I heard a slippered foot ascending the stairs; I listened and heard my room door open; I knew what was up then, and so I *started* for my room. I opened the door and step[p]ed in and found Doc Johnson seated very comfortably in an arm chair talking to my chum. I said "Good evening Doctor." "Good evening sir," was the reply. The old cock then proceeded to ask me concerning my studies, &c. I told him the necessary amount of lies, and he departed. I found however, that he had asked my chum several questions concerning my habits, &c; chum—who by the by is very religiously inclined— gave him a good account of me, and so I guess he is not much wiser than before his call. We had made arrangements to tick-tack the old hoss, that night, and so we determined to give it to him right.[13] We fastened the apparatus in the attic, and commenced about 11 o'clock after working for about a half-hour, and producing no Johnson, we held a council of war, and I was chosen to go to his room and see whether he was in.

Accordingly I ascended the steps and knocked at his door, and step[p]ed aside ready to run should he appear; he did not, and so I knocked again; this produced no response and so I kicked. After raising the devil generally, I came to the conclusion that Johnson was not in and that we, therefore, were sold. We did not mention *that* scrape to the rest of the stud's.

Now as I have written to you the longest letter that I *ever* wrote, and as I am rather tired of writing, I will close. Sending my respects for Lloyd, Dick,[14] Dutch, Hal,[15] and all other friends I am,

Very truly yours

Sing Ashenfelter

Particular P.S. Just give my pious regards to Emmie Ullman,[16] or [*sic*] and tell her that I will tend to her case when I get back to Phoenix.

13. Tick-tacks were small contraptions, typically made of wood or stones tied together with string. A prankster could attach the device to a door and, pulling the string from a distance, cause the rocks to hit the door, producing a "tick, tack" noise. Upon hearing the knock, the bewildered occupant would open the door to find no one in sight.

14. Richard Denithorne (1842–93) was a friend who participated in a political prank with SMA and SWP during a congressional election. See *Autobiography*, 82.

15. It is unclear who Dutch and Hal were. It is possible that Hal was SWP's younger brother, Henry Clay Pennypacker (1847–1922), or possibly a childhood friend named James Henry Workman.

16. Emiline Ullman, about fifteen years old, was the daughter of Lewis Ullman, a hotel-keeper in Phoenixville, where SWP once "paid ten cents" to see "a Chinaman, then on exhibition, as a *rara avis*." Emiline appears to have never married.

Do not let any one see this through whome its contents might reach Father.[17] Albert Shafer,[18] for instance.

SA

Dickinson College May 22nd [1862]

Dear Pennie,

Yours of the 14th inst. lies before me: I submit the following as an answer. As it is *devilish* hot, and as I, having thrown open the window, door, and ventilators, have, for the last half-hour, been sitting with head and legs projected from the former, in vain attempts to catch a breath of air, and at length, completely "bored," first, to d—n hot weather, and second, to write, have thrown myself into a seat, you must not expect this to compare in excellence with the letter to which it purports to be a reply.

"Assuredly" it gratifyeth my feelings exceeding much to know that my friends appreciate the merits of early rising; and verily it would afford me much pleasure, if I could feel assured that *they* put into practice that which they so much admire in others: wanting which assurance, I lack also the accompaning pleasures.

Your allusion to "Smike,"[19] although not altogether without 'point,' still, is minus consistancy; for you will find it utterly impossible to reconcile my character of "Joe" ("D—n that boy he's asleep again.") with one so much at varience with it, as "Smike": and if doubt should arise as to which I personate, by a reference to my form and habits, it will be readily be [*sic*] perceived that my similarity to the former gives the solution. But enough of this foolishness.

Pennie, I thank you sincerely for those remarks, for I know they were made with the most friendly feelings; but in reply, allow me to assure you that I did not act entirely without thought. I was a stranger to all except Shaffer, and wishing to get into good favor with my fellow students, I adopted the course which I thought would most readily produce that result. I think I am justifiable in saying that I succeeded in my design.

I have recitations in the following books: Ovid, Latin Grammar, Latin Prose (Arnolds), Geometry, Manuel of Classical Literature, Greek Reader and Grammar, Fowler's Rhetorical Forms, and Anatomy. The Greek Reader and Grammar

17. SMA's father, Henry Ashenfelter (1814–91), was a nail manufacturer and manager at the Phoenix Iron Company.

18. Albert Shafer (d. 1894) of Baltimore was a clerk for the Phoenix Iron Company.

19. Smike was a character in the novel *Nicholas Nickleby,* published as a serial from 1838 to 1839, by Charles Dickens (1812–70). In the story Smike is a simple boy who is frequently beaten up.

are not studied by the Freshman Class, I study them because I am behind in Greek; at present the class is reading Homer.[20] I expect to be up to them by next September. Your supposition that much attention is given to the languages is a correct one. My boarding is $2.50 per week washing $1.25 per month; but I will send you a Catalogue containing all the particulars and then you can judge for yourself.[21] The annual expenses are a little more than the Catalogue says, but still I think they are very cheap. I think, with a little study you could enter the Junior Class without much difficulty; you could make up all that would be nessary in two months. If you would come on next September and enter Junior, I do not think it would cost you over $250 to $500 to graduate, although it would depend a great deal on your habits. I think you could obtain a scholarship for two years for about $20.00, and then of course you would not have to pay tuition fees.

I am very sorry to hear that Ben[22] is sick, and I hope, when you answer this, you will be able to inform me of his recovery. It would have been better for him if he had never entered the army, but had kept on at school.

Bully for the "lecture tickets," and D—n Powers. Three cheers for Priestly and Mellon,[23] Three and a tiger[24] for the glorious old Y.M.L.U. "long may she wave[.]"

Bully for the girls, and Richard, luck to Little Mac,[25] and to the devil with his "plan," long live Greeley,[26] curse the cowardly 'rebs' thanks to Jake March,[27] regards to Lloyd, Dick, and all the rest, and I am

Very Truly Yours

Sing. Ashenfelter

20. See Appendix A for the college curriculum from this period.

21. See Appendix B for a summary of the costs involved with attending Dickinson College.

22. SWP's first cousin Benjamin R. Whitaker (1844–97) served in the 104th Pennsylvania Volunteers, the same regiment as SMA's older brother, George W. Ashenfelter (1840–77), who is mentioned in later letters.

23. It is unclear who Powers and Priestly were. Joseph C. Mellon (1845–1919) was elected treasurer of the YMLU in 1865. See Henry Clay Pennypacker to SWP, March 20, 1865, PM.

24. The exclamation "Three cheers and a tiger" was "an intensive form of applause; an addition thought to embellish the traditional three cheers." See John S. Farmer and William E. Henley, *A Dictionary of Slang and Colloquial English* (New York: G. Routledge and Sons, 1905), 476.

25. Maj. Gen. George B. McClellan (1826–85), known as "Little Mac," was leading the Union army up the Virginia Peninsula toward the Confederate capital of Richmond during the spring and early summer of 1862. The Peninsula Campaign would ultimately result in Union defeat.

26. Horace Greeley (1811–72) was the bombastic editor of the most influential Republican newspaper of the Civil War era, the *New York Tribune*.

27. Jacob M. March (1840–1913), a friend of SMA and SWP, served as a private in the 30th Pennsylvania Infantry from June 6, 1861, until he was discharged on June 13, 1864. Several letters from March are held in SWP's papers at PM.

P.S. I will answer Lloyds letter soon; tell him he must excuse me for not answering it first, as I wanted to give you the *particulars.* SA

[*Editors' Note:* Throughout his subsequent correspondence, Ashenfelter occasionally alludes to the five-dollar wager established in the following note.]

Phoenixville Aug 11th 1862

On the day of my marriage I promise to pay to the order of Saml. W. Pennypacker the sum of five dollars; providing said marriage take place before the 9th day of May 1884[.]

Sing Ashenfelter

Dickinson College Sept 28th 1862

Dear Sam,

At length, after delaying the matter almost a month I once more sit down to address you. Since my arrival here, I have not applied myself to study as strictly as I had expected. In fact, I dropped College, took up war, and started out as a "militia." The way of it was this. Heard that Pennsylvania was invaded.[28] Heard, moreover, that she appealed to her patriotic sons for defense. Great excitement in town: Everybody patriotic. Caught the prevalent feeling. Came up to College and wrote the following.

Hark! The bugle, loudly sounding,
Calls us from our task away.
Rattling drum and war horse bounding,
Tell us of the coming fray.
We must leave all other duty,
'Tis our country calls us now.
Rall[y]ing 'round our flag of beauty,
Hear an[d] register our vow.
By the blood of fallen heroes, by the power that reigns on high,
We will meet the base invaders, drive them back, or, fighting, die.

28. Confederate general Robert E. Lee invaded Maryland in September 1862, a campaign that resulted in the Battle of Antietam on September 17. The rumor SMA had heard was wrong. Lee's forces did not invade Pennsylvania in September, though Confederate cavalry under Maj. Gen. J. E. B. Stuart did venture north of the Mason-Dixon Line the following month.

Thought I had evinced sufficient patriotism, and consequently felt releived. Took a second thought and came to the conclusion to join the "milishe." Went down town and fixed my name to the roll. Began to feel enthusiastic. Company fell into ranks, and marched up to the depot amid cheers of the populace. At depot— order given "Company rest." Company rested, (in ranks,) for two hours. Began to grow tired of resting. Three hours. Mutiny began to be visible. Men straggling out of ranks. Recalled to duty by the whistle of the cars, which soon came to hand. Jumped aboard. Train started amid a profusion of cheers and tears. Arrived at Chambersburg, very cold. Waited about a half hour. Finally ordered to "Forward march." Marched three miles. Came to a woods and halted. Discovered that it was midnight and began to feel sleepy. Marched into the woods. Built fires and fixed up as comfortably as possible. Tried to sleep, too much noise. Tried again; another failure. Gave it up in despair and lay on my back, "star gazing" until day light. Rose up half frozen. Went up to the fire and warmed myself. Breakfast time. No rations had arrived. Forced to "chew the cud of sweet and bitter fancy" or starve. Chose the former and got the blues like thunder. Dinner time. Beef and bread just arrived. Took double rations, and consequently there was none left for supper. Went to work and built tents, from rails and straw. Discovered that it was Sunday, and the discovery occasioned us no little surprise. Went to bunk. Woke up next morning in fine spirits, but d—d cold. Plenty of grub. Spent four days in camp. Began to get used to it. Never liked anything better in my life. Woke up one morning and found myself discharged. The reason was as follows. About twenty students were in. Scotch[29] afraid College would break up. Petitioned Gov. Curtin[30] for our discharge. Gov. ordered it, and our militia service was over. There, I have taken up so much room with this one subject that I will hardly have sufficient [SMA crossed out "room" here] to write about anything more. However I have nothing more to say except to tell you the cause of my delay in writing to you & Lloyd. I wrote home several times, but, as I have since discovered, the replies were miscarried. I receiving none swore I would write none. I got my first letter from the office, the other day, and now begin once more to write. Sending my regards to Lloyd, Dick, and all the rest, I remain,

　　Truly Your Friend,
　　Sing.
I will write to Lloyd in a few days.

29. Scotch appears to be an unflattering nickname for Dickinson president Herman M. Johnson.

30. Andrew Gregg Curtin (1817–94), Dickinson class of 1837, was a conservative Republican governor of Pennsylvania from 1861 to 1867.

Dickinson College Nov. 22nd 1862

Dear Pennie,

Yours of the 2nd inst. now lies before me; having plenty of leisure time this evening, I will endeavor to reply. As you appear to be willing to make all sorts of acknowledgements in regard to your remissness in replying to my former letter, I, of course cannot do less than grant a ready pardon. But to tell the truth Pennie, if convenient to *you,* nothing would afford *me* more pleasure than frequent communication between us. Frequently, I become so bored with reading & study that I think a few more correspondents would be a god send. I dislike exceedingly to write two replies to one letter, or to address myself so frequently to a correspondent as to become borous, but if you can find the time to write I would be very glad to hear from you more frequently. And so you find a teacher's duties to be somewhat arduous.[31] Well, I can only say "go in" and deal out punishment in the same proportion as it was dealt when you were a youngster. Your actions relative to the draft were certainly very creditable.[32] I assure you that I am very glad that your Mother[33] was more active in the matter than yourself, as,

A private in Milish
Holds a very poor Posish.

At present, I am endeavoring to kill time by the perusal of Gil Blas.[34] I have come to the conclusion that, although it may be a very excellent work when printed in the French language, yet when rendered into English it consists of many very good ideas, thrown together, with a miserable lack of composition. I read it merely for the sake of curiosity.

31. SWP described his teaching duties in a letter to his uncle about this time: "I have quite a large school, in the neighborhood of 40 youngsters. Though most of them are quite small you may suppose they keep me pretty busy. So far I like it very well and have succeeded in keeping them in pretty good order. At first they were very noisy not having been accustomed to much discipline but they have generally learned better." SWP to Uncle, Oct. 16, 1862, PM.

32. The Militia Act of July 17, 1862, enabled the president to call the state militias into federal service and, if necessary, draft "able-bodied male citizens between the ages of eighteen and forty-five." SWP was drafted under this law but somehow managed to avoid service. See Joseph R. Whitaker to SWP, Oct. 21, 1862, and Juliann Elizabeth Whitaker to SWP, Oct. 29, 1862, both at PM. SWP later described being drafted in 1863 and hiring a substitute to avoid the service. See *Autobiography,* 97.

33. Anna Maria Whitaker Pennypacker (1815–99) lived most of her life in Phoenixville. She married Isaac A. Pennypacker in 1839.

34. French playwright and novelist Alain-René Lesage (1668–1747) published the picaresque novel *Gil Blas* in four volumes between 1715 and 1735.

One of the greatest advantages which College affords, apart from study, is an opportunity for a regular course of reading. In connection with Dickinson, there are libraries containing in all about 25000 volumes, and there is therefor no difficulty whatever in always having interesting matter on hand.

I had a slight difficulty with the Faculty a short time ago. They accused three of us of plug[g]ing the bell room and thus interfering with recitations. We pleaded innocent but all to no purpose, for they assessed upon us the damages done to the bell room door, and took 400 marks from each of our class standings. My most intimate College friend is Lan Himes[35] alias "Giglamps" of whome, no doubt, you have heard me speak. Last Saturday morning he & I started on a trip to his home: we walked the whole distance—twenty seven miles—and arrived at our destination at 3.30 P.M. We had a gay time & returned to Carlisle on Tuesday evening. As you will see, we are neighbors. He is a bully boy. It is now about half past eleven o'clock, and I must retire as I have been up very late for the past few nights.

Believe me

Your True Friend

Sing Ashenfelter

P.S. Give my kindest regards to all the boys.

S.

[*Editors' Note:* According to the faculty minutes of November 3, 1862, "Ashenfelter & [William B.] McClure and J. B. Bowman were reported by the President as guilty of having broken into the bell room." The faculty "decided that the damages should be divided between them & that they be assessed 400 minus marks apiece with the understanding that these should not affect their connection with the College."

On November 10 Ashenfelter appeared before the faculty and "stated that on the morning on which the bell room was plugged, he was down town & did not return to West College until the time of ringing the bell (after 9 A.M.). This was Saturday morning, & on leaving for breakfast, he did [not] return till after 9. He stopped in [Charles J.] String's room, till after the time for ringing the bell." String's testimony coincided with everything that Ashenfelter claimed. Wilbur Burnite then testified "that he returned with Ashenfelter via Hospital & upon

---

35. James Lanius Himes (1845–81) of New Oxford, Pennsylvania, graduated from Dickinson in 1865 and was admitted to the bar in York, Pennsylvania, in 1868 before moving to Minneapolis, Minnesota, in 1869. He served two terms as a city justice in Minneapolis. For more on Himes, see the introduction.

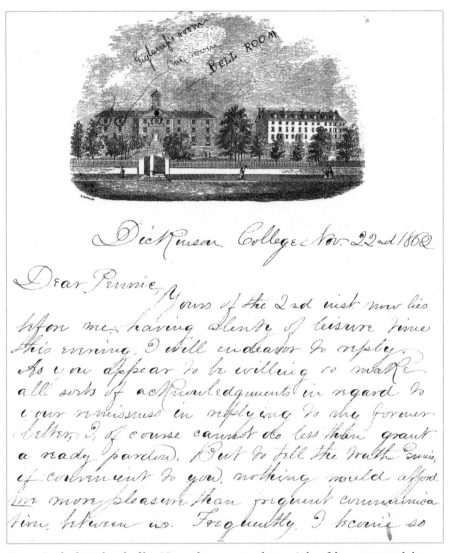

Fig. 11. In the letterhead of his November 22, 1862, letter, Ashenfelter annotated the image of West College by pointing out the locations of his room, James Himes's room, and the bell room. (Courtesy of Pennypacker Mills, County of Montgomery, Schwenksville, PA)

returning to Burnite's (String's) room remained there until it was remarked that the bell ought to ring. It was then after 9." Next, Vosburg Shaffer stated that "on the Sat. morning in question he went to Mr. Burnite's room and staid there until the bell should ring. Also before breakfast he was with Ashenfelter from the time they rose." Shaffer further "testified that on another occasion he & Mr. Ashenfelter had passed by the bell room door & found it plugged, but they themselves had nothing to do with it. As to ringing the bell at night Mr. Shaffer testified that he was awoke by the noise & found his chum in bed." Ashenfelter then stated "that at one time passing the door of the bell room he noticed a plug in it & as he happened to have a hatchet in his hand he struck it as he passed. He denies positively having been engaged in breaking into the attic in the first section. E.C." A few other students also testified.

After the students left the room, Dr. Johnson "presented the Testimony of several of the most reliable students that they had seen the students in question engaged in plugging the door. He also presented a paper from a reliable student in the first section of East College, who gave the names of those concerned in tearing up the planks in the first section, Ashenfelter, Bowman, and [Alfred M.] Rhoads." The faculty then "decided that the damages therefore in E. Coll. first section be divided between these three."[36]]

36. The bell room had been a favorite site for pranks by students. See Charles Coleman Sellers, *Dickinson College: A History* (Middleton, CT: Wesleyan Univ., 1973), 243.

CHAPTER TWO

1863

Dick. Coll. Feb. 12th 1863

Dear Pennie,

I dont know what the truth may be, but there is a lingering idea somewhere about the inner recesses of my cranium to the effect that your correspondent at Dick. may justly be accused of being dilatory. If by any chance or combination of circumstances, this above-mentioned idea may be able to rejoice in sufficient foundation to afford it establishment as a certainty then the said correspondent begs leave to offer the well known fact that indolence is one of his prominent characteristics, as an excuse for the delay. My Chum, who, in imagination transformed into an Eastern juggler, has, for the past half hour, been amusing himself by the exhibition of skillful feats in knife-throwing, to the great detriment of our black-board, is, I think a youth of sufficient consequence to merit a description in this interesting (?) letter.[1] Imagine a young man, who, in height, is somewhere between five and six feet; with a form neither very slender nor remarkably stout; eyes, which, excepting as regards color, differ in no wise from any other eyes; a nose which has an entirely opposite tendency from that of your correspondent; lips which present the appearance of having been constructed for the purpose of speaking, affording a covering to the teeth, and whistling "Yankee Doodle"; and hair, the color & appearance of which do not in the least resemble Lloyds whiskers;—imagine this I say, and you will have just about as good an idea of Mr. Jas B Bowman, as you had before you received this description.

There! I guess that is about enough of d—d nonsense for one letter. You recollect that during vacation I was speaking to you of Poe's "Descent into the

1. SMA included the notation "(?)" in the text.

31

Maelstrom.["]² You can find it on the 542nd page of (vol 2nd) Cyclopedia of American Literature, in the library of Y.M.L.U.³

A few days after my return to "Old Dick" I commenced reading Rollin.⁴ But, after finishing the histories of the Egyptians and of the Carthaginians, I came to the conclusion that I would defer the further perusal of that interesting work until some future period. I have just finished "Pluribusta" by Doesticks. It is a parody of Longfellows "Hiawatha" and some parts of it are very good.⁵ I am now reading De Quincy's "Confessions of an opium eater."⁶ It is one of those strangely written works which one cannot but like. He calls opium "the dread agent of inconceivable pleasure and pain."

I find it impossible to make this letter any longer as I can find nothing to write about. When you reply, give me your idea of what a correspondence *should* be. I think that between friends it should not be confined to the mere dry statement of facts, but should include the interchanging of ideas upon those things which interest both.

Hoping you will not be as tardy in answering as I in writing I remain
Your Friend
Sing Ashenfelter

                                        Dickinson, March 4th. 1863

Dear Pennie,

As you are a young man of steady habits, I have no doubt that you would be exceedingly horrified if you were within the precincts of Dickinson College to night. One who has never been in the habit of associating with "*sportive* youths"

---

2. Edgar Allan Poe (1809–49) published the short story "A Descent into the Maelstrom" in 1841.

3. The Young Men's Literary Union provided its members access to a collection of books and newspapers as well as regular discussions and debates. SWP recalled in his autobiography that the YMLU "helped me very much to gain self-possession and develop the capacity for public speech."

4. Probably French historian Charles Rollin (1661–1741), who wrote *Traité des Etudes* (1726–31), *Histoire Ancienne* (1730–38), and *Histoire Romaine* (1739–50; completed by J. B. L. Crevier).

5. New York humorist Mortimer Thomson (1832–75) wrote under the pseudonym Q. C. Philander Doesticks. Shortly after Henry Wadsworth Longfellow (1807–82) published *The Song of Hiawatha* (1855), Thomson published a parody entitled *Plu-Ri-Bus-Tah: A Song That's-By-No-Author* (New York: Livermore and Rudd, 1856).

6. English essayist Thomas De Quincey (1785–1859) wrote *Confessions of an English Opium-Eater* in 1822.

cannot possibly imagine the din which is raised by a party of students "on a tight." Once every year, each of our literary societies elect one cheif & five subordinate orators to represent them in their anniversaries at the College Commencement, & it being customary for the cheif speaker elect to "stand treat" on the evenings of their elections we have, as a natural result, any quantity of drunken students at that time. Last Wednesday the Union Philosophical Society held such an election, &, in the evening of that day the above mentioned result duly followed. To day, the Belles Letters Soc. held theirs, & we have a repetition of the scene.[7] I however, have had sufficient *moral courage* to refrain from drinking at both times, & consequently have the pleasure of addressing you this evening. We had an exciting time in our society to day. Two of the members, who last Wednesday were elected as speakers, resigned their positions because their candidate for the cheif speakership had not been elected, & the arrangements did not suit them. They did this in so disrespectful a manner that several of us arose & "gave them thunder[.]" The affair almost ended in a fight at the time; it is not yet settled as we intend to have one of the resigning parties arraigned for insulting the society. The excitement in the Y.M.L.U. at the time of the Lecture Committee rumpus was no circumstance to this.

March 8th,

Although I began this letter several days ago, I had no opportunity of completing it until now. My abrupt breaking off on last Wednesday evening was caused by the entrance of one of the speakers elect, who insisted upon me going down town & assisting at an oyster supper given by Wm. D. Clayton,[8] the Belles Letters Anniversarian; I went.

I have no doubt that the R. Room is a paragon of cleanliness; for I believe you & Lloyd would devote your lives to sweeping & dusting, rather than endure a few hours of "dirty magnificence." The actions of Smith & Powers[9] outside of the Y.M.L.U. go to prove that we held them in the true estimation there, I would not fret myself over any misfortune that might happen to either. Since I last wrote to you I have finished reading "Somebody's Luggage,"[10] (Dickens last) &

---

7. The Union Philosophical Society, founded at Dickinson College in 1789, and the Belles Lettres Literary Society, founded in 1786, are two of the oldest collegiate literary societies in the United States.

8. William Daily Clayton (1838–1909) of Saint Louis, Missouri, graduated from Dickinson College on June 25, 1863. Following graduation, he enlisted in the Confederate army.

9. It is unclear who Smith and Powers were or what they had done.

10. British novelist Charles Dickens (1812–70) published *Somebody's Luggage* in 1862, a short novel about a waiter who publishes stories he discovers in abandoned luggage at a hotel.

one of Miss Muloch's works, entitled John Halifax, Gent.[11] I do not think that the former is "anything to brag on" although it comes from Dickens. The latter is very good; it is as true a description of a gentleman as one would wish to read.

As you say, any one will feel a slight hesitation in committing all his thoughts to paper; & I think this is especially the case with those who desire to fill an honorable political position in the future. I think, however, that we can trust eachother never to take advantage of any thing written now: & if we carry on so open a correspondence, it will, of course, be between none but ourselves; for we might give expression to some thoughts which it would not be pleasant to own before others. As you mention religious subjects first in your suggestions, I will give my opinions upon the same. In the first place I do not regard the Bible as a work of Divine inspiration; but rather as a result of over excited brains; We have had so called prophets & inspired writers in all ages & I consider that we owe as much veneration to the writings of Mahomut as those of Moses; to the Koran as to the Bible, & the sayings of Joe Smith[12] are not one whit inferior to those of John the Baptist. I admire the Bible as a teacher of morality but no more. This lack of belief in the *Book of Books* implies of course an equal doubt in the divinity of Christ. I do not think a *son* of God is possible: neither do I believe an infinite being would create a world, knowing how much misery would accrue therefrom, & knowing also that he would have to give *his own son* for its redemption. The whole doctrin[e] of Christianity seems to me unnatural. I do believe though in a supreme being, a creator & governor of the universe; I believe it to be our duty as inferior beings to worship him and to act in such a manner as he may require. I believe the knowledge of right & wrong is natural to every one, & if we do as conscience directs our future existence will be free from all trouble & care. As to what the future life will be I can only surmise. No *human* being ever knew what came after death & I do not think any one will ever possess that knowledge. We can only trust in our Creator. Such is a portion of my religious views, & although they are not the articles of a popular faith, I feel that I can safely trust them as the truest disciple of Christ can his. It is dinner time now & I must close

Remaining
Truly Yours
Sing Ashenfelter
P.S. Regards to all
S

When you reply put, Box 222, on the envelope

11. Dinah Mulock Craik, *John Halfax, Gentleman* (1856).
12. Joseph Smith (1805–44) founded the Church of Latter Day Saints in 1830.

Dickinson, May 30th 1863

Dear Pennie,

I once heard a young man complaining of a negligent correspondent; to writing to whome he expressed a strong reluctance on account of the irregularity of his replies. I wrote to you on the 8th of last March & received a reply on the 22nd of April. I could account for these six weeks of delay only by the supposition that you did not wish to be bored so frequently by my epistles. Accordingly, I have taken the time of your delay as an index for my own; & this will account for your not having heard from me sooner.

I entirely agree with you, as regards the injury inflicted upon Y.M.L.U. by the withdrawal of that remarkable skeleton; the old room must really look unnatural without it. I regard the owner of that collection of old bones as but little better than a brainless fool. And I believe that at heart, he is a d—d traitor. What I say of *him*, in this respect, I say of all who wear those infernal copperheads; & prefer the expression, "I am a Democrat" to "I am for the restoration of the Union."[13] Traitors, one & all. I am very much obliged to you for having an eye to my interest, as regards that old book; your mentioning the matter reminds me of the fact that I have not, as yet, taken out the worth of the eight dollars & ten cents, of which old "Scotch" ["]euchered" me. I must make another excursion.

Until within the last month I had thought that Dickens was, without doubt, the finest novelist that ever wrote. I have had reason to change my opinion. I have read Victor Hugo's "Les Miserables."[14] I am not in the habit of growing enthusiastic over the works of any author; but I must say, for this book, that it has produced a deeper impression upon me than any other that I ever read. The delineation of the two principal characters,—Jean Valjean an escaped & a reformed convict, & Javert, a French detective,—I regard as grand surpassing description. It is my intention to reread it at my earliest possible convenience. I have read thus far in my Sophomore year, upwards of 10,000 pages without taking my recitations into account which in themselves would amount to between 1,000 & 2,000 additional. I am now reading "The Life & Writings of Edgar A. Poe["]; & I find them exceedingly curious & interesting. Our Libraries here afford rare facilities for any one who has a desire to become "well read.["] In the three—the College, the U.P.S. & B.L.S.—there are about 24000 volumes, & additions are constantly being made. I regard them as the best part of the whole institution.

13. "Copperhead" was an epithet used by Republicans during the Civil War to denote Democrats as disloyal traitors. It is unknown to whom SMA is referring here, although it may have been either Smith or Powers, mentioned above.

14. French novelist, poet, and playwright Victor Hugo (1802–85) published *Les Miserables* in 1862.

We come now, to use your own expression, to the consideration of the religious subjects which have been discussed. I find that on this point we do not essentially differ. We agree in prefering common sense & our own knowledge of right & wrong to the worn out records of a superstitious age—in the recognition of an omnipotent power, a creator & governor of the universe—& in regarding the future as inscrutable.

You say that, while you doubt the divinity of the Bible, you cannot see what good would result from its overthrow. As far as regards the *present* condition of the world & its inhabitants you are undoubtedly correct; but cannot you conceive of a faith which would be more perfectly adapted to the temporal *future?* What do you suppose the old Romans or Greeks, the firm believers in ancient mythology would have anticipated as the result of the overthrow of the religion of their day? Would not general prophecies of some dreadful result have accompanied all ideas of such an overthrow. And yet we see that there are scarcely any vestiges of that faith left standing. Every age has its peculiarities. And why is it unnatural to suppose that Christianity is a characteristic of the present? The doctrines which the Bible inculcates to-day is no greater improvement upon Mythology than is Civilization upon Barbarism. As the world has improved its popular faith has kept pace with it & the right to look forward to a more advanced civilization which will displace the present with the supposition that the reconciliation is thus rendered perfect. It appears a little curious to me that this should be the stopping point. Why not go a little further? It is because beyond that point the "records of the rocks" cannot possibly be made to agree with the records of the Old Testament. The Bible is usually regarded as a work of inspiration; if so, as coming from a truthful God, it should contain nothing but indisputable truth. Is this the case? Geology proves beyond the shadow of a doubt that the creation of the various types of the Animal as well as Vegetable Kingdom took place at vastly different periods. Thus, some species of plants, some of fishes, & some of terrestrial animals were created in one period, & other species of the same in another: & the creations in each period are so intermingled that they must have been almost simultaneous. The Bible says that these plants, fishes, & animals, each were created at different periods, & moreover, that every species of each was created at the same time. The idea is somewhat difficult to understand, as it is expressed above. Words are the better medium for the expression of ideas.

I have lengthened this letter, already, beyond what I had intended, & as my time is taken up for the rest of the day, I will close.

Your Friend

Sing Ashenfelter

[*Editors' Note:* Ashenfelter was at home in Phoenixville for the summer when the Confederates invaded Pennsylvania in June 1863. As Robert E. Lee's men headed north, Governor Curtin issued a proclamation calling for men to enlist in military units during the emergency. Pennypacker rushed to Phoenixville one night after working in the fields and proposed to some of his friends "to go up to Harrisburg and unite with some company there, as there was but little prospect of one being raised in our own neighborhood." Horace Lloyd "seemed to think well of it" but could not give a definite answer until he spoke with his boss. Early the next morning Pennypacker returned to town and found it "in a perfect furore of excitement." He went to Lewis Ullman's hotel and found Vosburg Shaffer "writing down the names of recruits rapidly." In a burst of enthusiasm, Pennypacker told him to add his name to the list.

Later that day Pennypacker boarded a train for Harrisburg. Singleton and George Ashenfelter, Lloyd, and Pennypacker's cousin, Andrew R. Whitaker, joined too, although the last did so without his mother's consent. The Ashenfelter brothers do not appear to have gone with the intent to enlist.

In Harrisburg the boys and their informal company camped out around the state capitol. When it started raining they went inside, and a few of them slept inside the chamber of the state house of representatives. The next day the boys did some drilling and ate their first army rations. "Did yours smell bad?" Lloyd asked his companions. The other boys realized that he had been given "an offensive spoiled piece which he was uncomplainingly endeavoring to force down." "Well," said Lloyd, "I thought I was in the army and had to eat it." Pennypacker recalled that his friend said this "with such an air of innocence and resignation that it threw us all into a roar of laughter. He hasn't heard the last of it yet."

After drilling, Whitaker, Lloyd, and Pennypacker went with their company's captain to see Governor Curtin. "At the Capitol we met Sing. Ashenfelter who accompanied us. While there we took the opportunity of 'drawing' some envelopes from the Governor's private box. Afterward we four walked about town for a time, when Sing left us promising to come out to camp in the afternoon."

The next day after drill, Lloyd, Ashenfelter, Whitaker, and Pennypacker again went into Harrisburg, where they crossed "over the tottering wooden bridge which spans the Susquehanna, climbed up the very steep hill on the western bank of that river, upon which [a large group of men] were busily engaged throwing up fortifications." They watched the men work for a while. Ashenfelter afterward caught a train for Carlisle, while the other three returned to camp.

Soon the boys learned that they would need to be mustered into the state service in order to receive arms, equipment, clothing, and pay. Unfortunately, they could not find enough Phoenixville men to form a full company, so Lloyd and Whitaker decided to return home. Pennypacker, however, joined Company F of the 26th Pennsylvania Emergency Militia, a unit consisting primarily of men from Pottstown. He spent most of the next few weeks in this regiment.[15] The Battle of Gettysburg took place July 1–3, 1863. Pres. Abraham Lincoln visited the battlefield a few months later, on November 19, to participate in the dedication of the national cemetery there.]

Dickinson College
Nov 22nd. 1863.

Dear Sam,

I have so much to write about in this letter; so many stray thoughts to collect & note; so many different subjects to treat of; & withal so little time to do it in, that I scarcely know where to begin. However, as the minor topics of consideration require the least effort of thought, & as I specially desire to reserve whatever brains I do possess for the clearer presentation of my ideas upon a subject which I am beginning to regard as all important, I will proceed to give you, in detail, whatever comments on miscellaneous matters may suggest themselves to me. I perceive from yours of the 19th inst., that you are liable to draw an unwarrantable conclusion; or rather inference. I assure you, it would take more than a long silence on your part to give me offense; for while I certainly did regret your delay, that feeling was tinged with nothing of bitterness. I determined, however, to return the compliment; & in so doing I believe I overstepped, by a few days, the proscribed time. I was surprised into a knowledge of this fact by the letter which I received a few days since.

Previous to its receipt, I had not been aware that Andy[16] had taken up quarters at West Chester. My facilities for obtaining news from Phoenixville are not so great as you imagine. Lloyd writes but about once in every three or four weeks; Andy is still worse; & my letters from home contain very little, except

---

15. SWP, *Six Weeks in Uniform: Being the Record of a Term in the Military Service of the United States in the Gettysburg Campaign of 1863* (Schwenksville, PA: Pennypacker Mills, n.d.), 1–11. On the morning of July 4, SMA, Richard Denithorne, Horace Lloyd, Andrew R. Whitaker, and a few others went out on a target-shooting excursion. SMA's mother, Catharine, went to Gettysburg with several other people to deliver supplies for Union soldiers. See Horace Lloyd to SWP, July 24, 1863, PM.

16. Andrew R. Whitaker (1845–1917) was cousin of SWP and brother of Benjamin R. Whitaker. In his autobiography SWP calls him "not only a relative but a staunch friend." Later as governor, SWP appointed Whitaker a member of the Pennsylvania Fish Commission.

information relative to family matters. Indeed, although your letter was written in Philadelphia, it contained more Phoenixville news than any other which I have received this session.

As you seem to be interested in that "very expressive expression," "Let 'em flutter," I will venture an explanation. We Dickinsonions, in desiring to exhibit a hearty, though somewhat careless sense of approval, give vent to our feelings in that—to you—misterious phraze. But why, in mentioning the subject, did you so studiously avoid all allusion to that which occasioned the remark in my letter to Lloyd? Ah! Sam, I fear that my information in regard to a certain matter in which you are nearly concerned, is but too correct. I fear that, were the facilities for obtaining information as great in one case as in the other, Lloyd could couple your name with that of a certain young lady in N.Y. in just as interesting a manner as you couple his with Eliza's.[17] After telling of the proposed movement of Annie Euen,[18] you say: "However, I suppose you have been informed in regard to that movement, long ago." Now, in the first place, I give you my word that I knew nothing of the matter, previous to the receipt of your letter. I never have been in correspondence with Annie, & I never expect to be. You will doubtless recollect that, at one time, I told you of my feelings towards the young lady. When I inform you that those feelings have undergone no change, but rather, have been strengthened by time; that I have positive knowledge (Her own assurances.) that they are reciprocated, you will perhaps wonder why this silence exists between us. You may have gathered from my remarks in regard to Dave Euen,[19] something which will throw light upon the matter. If not, I will tell you frankly; He will not allow it. Dave Euen dislikes me, & I assure you there is no love lost in that quarter. While I hate him for what he has done, I also thank him.

17. Mary Eliza "Lide" Vanderslice (1843–81) married Horace Lloyd in April 1865. In late 1862 Irvin J. Brower observed, "Lloyd and Lide are getting along fine they are together now about seven times a week and doubtless enjoy each others company very much." Brower to SWP, Oct. [n.d.] 1862, PM. Lide's father, John Vanderslice, was a wealthy real-estate developer and, according to one historian, "may have been the most hated man in Phoenixville" because of his practices for making money off of renters. Douglas R. Harper, *"If Thee Must Fight": A Civil War History of Chester County, Pennsylvania* (West Chester, PA: Chester County Historical Society, 1990), 32–33. It is unknown who the "certain young lady" from New York was.

18. Annie J. Euen (1846–1926) of Phoenixville grew up to be a music teacher and never married. She attended Vassar College in New York as a special student in 1865–66 but never matriculated. SWP's cousin, Ellen R. Whitaker, wrote: "It may be that Miss Euen is the attraction in Phoenixville. I suppose a year or two will determine whether I am right or wrong." Ellen R. Whitaker to SWP, Feb. 20, 1867, PM. The family name is sometimes spelled "Ewen" in the historical records.

19. Dr. David Euen (1820–87), father of Annie, owned a drugstore in Phoenixville. In April 1861 Abraham Lincoln appointed him deputy postmaster in Phoenixville.

Fig. 12. Anna J. Euen. (Courtesy of Pennypacker Mills, County of Montgomery, Schwenksville, PA)

Fig. 13. David Euen. (Courtesy of Pennypacker Mills, County of Montgomery, Schwenksville, PA)

I have made up my mind that these sheets shall show me to you, just as I am; & so I write what I would let no other person know. I am inordinately ambitious. The sentiment, "I would sooner rule in Hell, than serve in Heaven,"[20] expresses my feelings more fully than anything else I have ever read. If, in my future life, it ever happens that sentiment, predjudice, or even principle, stand opposed to my advancement, I drop them. I worship nothing but this God[d]ess Ambition. If I ever marry, it must be for wealth; for influence. Understand me though, I would not give a turn of my hand for wealth, in itself considered: I would desire it only as a means for the promotion of my ends. Perhaps you can understand now why I thank David as well as hate him. Perhaps, though you will also despise the sentiments which I have expressed. I would be very sorry if such should be the case, but it is just the way I feel; &, as I made up my mind to write to you honestly, I will endeavor to do so. I deem it due myself, though, again to state, that I would so express myself to no one but yourself. I have *very few* beliefs or sentiments which I would like to announce publicly.

I was very much surprised when I first heard that you had commenced the

20. This quotation comes from John Milton's *Paradise Lost* (1667).

Fig. 14. Singleton M. Ashenfelter, standing.
(Courtesy of Pennypacker Mills, County
of Montgomery, Schwenksville, PA)

study of law. I believe I never regretted anything more in my life than that you were prevented from returning with me to Dickinson. I regretted it principally on your account, of course, but I was somewhat selfish in the matter, too: for I am confident that a congenial spirit here would have done me a vast amount of good. You cannot imagine how much pleasure & gratification, arising from our social thought mingling, I had promised myself. Sometimes I almost imagine I will go mad if I cannot have some one, between whome, & myself, a mutual interchange of thought will not be a mutual bore. It is at such moments that I miss most just such a friend as I feel you to be. I turn to my chum, with whome, of all the students, I have most congeniality, but I always feel that something is lacking. The satisfaction which I desire is not so unalloyed as I could wish—there is something about it which palls. But, to return, while I thus regret the circumstances which deprived you of so much benefit, & me of so much pleasure, I cannot but rejoice to see you started in the noble profession. I congratulate you upon it, for I feel confident that you will succeed. I only wish I felt as sure of myself.

It seems to me, to night, as if the connections which I have formed at College are frail as thread when brought into comparison with my anterior friendships. I have a miserable, longing desire for some thing in the friendship here, which I feel should exist, but which I cannot find. When I look back at the evenings spent in the old room; when I ruminate over the tender recollections connected therewith; when, in short, I indulge in "Reveries"; I feel that perhaps there is more in Friendship than its admirers & advocates contend for. I joined the Society when I was but fourteen; & a sense of gratitude enhances my feelings towards it. I know that, had I been debarred of its privileges, my career so far would have been vastly different. It is the Society that I thank for my present position; for my truest feelings of friendship; & my dearest recollections. Perhaps, however, "absence lends to all a charm"; & you, who are so frequently within those four walls, cannot understand, or appreciate my feelings. If this be so, I ask you, give them, at least, the credit of being real.

You give me a quotation from Rousseau,[21] with the statement that you dont see the point. I must say I cannot see it either. Do you recollect, Ike Marvel,[22] in his "Reveries" upon reading, over the sea coal fire, says that over Rousseau, you lose yourself in a mental dream land, & are subjected to the influences of soul-music & soul culture. It was the name of the latter, in yours of the 19th., that called the expression to my mind, & in it I perceive I have somewhat anticipated myself. I *have* read "Reveries of a Bachelor," & I admire it very much. There is, published, a work by the same author, called "Dream Life";[23] which contains as true an expression of the sentiments of our younger, of our present days, as I have ever met. Everything is carried on in a tender undercurrent, & is so true withal, that one cannot but be charmed.

Speaking of of [*sic*] books, I will here express my opinions of "Shoulder Straps," by saying that if Henry Morford cannot do better at novel writing he had better take to boot blacking.[24] Its only redeeming feature is that it concerns

21. Enlightenment philosopher Jean-Jacques Rousseau (1712–78) authored several influential works, including *A Discourse on the Arts and Sciences* (1750) and *Discourse on the Origin and Basis of Inequality among Men* (1754).

22. Writing under the penname Ike Marvel, Donald Grant Mitchell (1822–1908) was an American novelist whose *Reveries of a Bachelor* (New York: Baker and Scribner, 1850) launched his career.

23. Ike Marvel, *Dream Life: A Fable of the Seasons* (1851).

24. Henry Morford (1823–81) wrote several novels about the Northern home front during the Civil War. *Shoulder-Straps* went through five editions and was reviewed positively in the press, unlike SMA's response to it. Historian J. Matthew Gallman explains that the concept of "shoulder straps" referred to officers in the army who "were soldiers, but in name only. These were the war's new breed of confidence men, now operating under the guise of the Union cause rather than the banner of individualism." Such officers, the *Philadelphia Inquirer* reported, "sport their tinseled uniform and blazing shoulder-straps on promenade; sleeping at the 'best hotels,' and enjoying costly liquors and wines, while their men have been neglected." J. Matthew Gallman, *Defining Duty in the Civil War: Personal Choice, Popular Culture, and the Union Home Front* (Chapel Hill: Univ. of North Carolina Press, 2015), 19, 70, 82–87.

the present day. By far the best work I have read this session is "Beulah[.]" It was written by Agusta J. Evans.[25] I will make no comments upon it. I simply wish you to read it, if you have not already done so. I think you will feel amply repaid.

I am forced to acknowledge that your proposition to carry on a part of our correspondence in French would meet with my most hearty approval, were it not for one circumstance: viz., the incapacity of your humble servant.[26] We have, lately, devoted our time entirely to translating; & that requires so little use of the grammar, that I would find great difficulty in writing even the exercises. I will study up, however, & if ever I am sufficiently advanced to warrant the attempt I will adopt your suggestion.

Strange as it may seem to you, I hardly devote to study a sufficient time for the getting our [out?] of my recitations. I hurry through in order to have a sufficient time for reading. I burn the midnight oil, but it is over Shak[e]speare, Dante, Butler or kindred spirits. (But I must I must [sic] stop & make another pen, as this is entirely worn out.) Sometimes I become so deeply interested as to neglect almost everything else. I find that I am beginning to think. When I first came to Dickinson I imagined that I was a pretty smart boy; & when praised for some silly scribbles which I wrote for the College bulletin board, I had the egotism to congratulate myself upon it. I am beginning to feel differently. I partially understand now what an educated man must be; & if my course at College suffices to teach me my own ignorance, it will have done enough—the time will have been well spent.

About two-thirds of the students went over to Gettysburg the other day, but I was not of the number.[27] We had petitioned the Faculty for holiday in order that we might be without restraint on that occasion: they refused to grant our request, but gave leave of absence to those who desired to go over. We who stayed in Carlisle united & refused to go to recitations until the others had returned. Dr. Johnson was not in the best of humors over the matter, but we were determined, & stood firm. The absent ones returned yesterday, & all is now right again.

Although, as you say, those notes which we exchanged, some time since,

25. Augusta Jane Evans (1835–1909) was an American author whose novel *Beulah* (New York: Derby and Jackson, 1859) explores the life of a young woman who struggled with skepticism about the Christian faith. The novel sold over 22,000 copies within a year of its publication. SMA quotes from it several times in subsequent letters.

26. SWP appears to have relished opportunities to read and converse in French, although he may not have been very competent. Once in 1863, during a long train ride, he "sat on the same seat with a Frenchman, and undertook to ask him some questions in his own language, but only on repeated reiterations could I make him understand a word, so I gave it up for a bad job." SWP to Aunt, Oct. 18, 1863, PM.

27. Gettysburg is about thirty miles south of Carlisle.

may be in opposition to the spirit of the law, & consequently, invalid, still, if you do not object, I would wish to regard them as binding. The spirit in which they were given was such as will render it almost impossible, I anticipate, for any question to arise, regarding their legality. I never knew, until your letter informed me, that Clem Lloyd[28] was a church member. I suppose that, with all the religious influences to which you are subjected, it will not be a great while ere you are enrolled among the elect. Clem certainly has a higher sense than I of the proper mode of spending the Sabbath. I never attend church now & very seldom persuade myself to look into the Bible. I cannot do either without feeling utterly disgusted at the superstition which supports so blind a beliefe, & accordingly I leave them alone.

I have met here at College a man whome I would call a genius. I will tell you something of his history as it was told me from his own lips. When quite a boy he served as clerk in the store of an old quaker lady in Wilmington, Del. He became so careless, however, that the old lady, after repeated warnings, finally turned him off; & he was left to shift for himself. He started for Philadelphia, & failing to obtain employment there, went on to New York, where he arrived in the middle of a cold night in December. He was ignorant of the city; & so spent the rest of the night wandering about. During the remainder of the winter, he peddled patent knife cleaners about the streets by day, & each night spent all that he earned[.] He slept in a miserable hovel at the Five Points.[29] In the spring, he returned again to Wilmington; where [he] apprenticed himself to a printer & determined to learn the trade. If you read the life of Horace Greeley, you will find that, when a boy at the case, he was visited by a terrible affliction known as the printers sore.[30] It is engendered by much standing & bad blood. Jackson,[31] the student I allude to, had just such a disease, with the addition of a severe rhumetism; & his sufferings, as he served papers in this condition must have been awful. Frequently, his limbs would give way, his papers be scattered over the ground, & himself made the subject of ridicule. This, he said, was the bitterest feeling he ever experienced,—to see people making sport of his misfortunes. Then he thought of suicide: but his better nature prevailed, & he made up his mind to raise himself.

28. Clement E. Lloyd (1843–1911), younger brother of Horace, was a member of the Young Men's Literary Union. He was baptized on April 6, 1862, at Old Saint Paul's Roman Catholic Church in Philadelphia.

29. Five Points is an old New York City neighborhood notorious in the nineteenth century for high levels of crime.

30. For Greeley's discussion of his sore leg, see J. Parton, *The Life of Horace Greeley, Editor of the New York Tribune* (New York: Mason Brothers, 1855), 103, 109.

31. J. W. Jackson is listed in the Dickinson College catalog as hailing from Wilmington, Delaware. A member of the class of 1866, he never graduated.

About this time, he caught hold of Scott's Novels;[32] & they, he said, showed him what he needed. They gave his thoughts altogether a new turn, & he determined to obtain an education. This was about three years since. Previous to that time, he could scarce read & write—he had not even the elements of an education. In these three years he has brought himself up to the highest position in the Sophomore class. He studies only three hours in the day, & yet his recitations are made almost verbatim. Moreover, in this time, he has made himself the best read fellow I ever met. His power of memory is absolutely marvelous. He can quote page after page from almost any author you may mention. I have, at times, been so carried away by his conversation that I could do nothing but sit & listen. But his great genius is shewn in his writings. Young as he is, he has written some things which I would be almost willing to rank among the best I ever read. If you can obtain the New York Mercury for Oct. 4th. 1862, & Aug. 8th. 1863,[33] you will see some things, which he blames himself for ever publishing, as he says they were not worth it. The one is entitled the "Demon Despair," & the other is the first poem in the paper. The former is somewhat lengthy & is written under the "nom de plum" of Maurice Mellnot. I think it is an excellent mingling of two of our best American poets. The latter, he wrote under his own name; (J. Jackson) & I think you will find it differing in arrangement from any thing else you ever saw.

I suppose, though, you have been considerably bored by this long digression; but I am so deeply interested in this Jackson that I could not refrain from telling you of him. His religious, or rather, psychological views, almost coincide with my own. I must say that in your first letter you threw out quite a weighty argument in support of the Bible. But, even admitting your train of reasoning to be perfect, I question whether we should allow an abstract syllogism to convince us of the utility or wisdom of that which reason teaches us to be folly. But must we admit your conclusion? Does mans apparently helpless, or rather dependent condition necessitate a guidance of this sort, from the hand of omnipotence? I think not. If the Creator desires that his influence shall be felt, he implants within the created intellectual faculties, subject to that influence. You say it would be unnatural to create, endow with faculties, &c. & then not give something indicative of his will. The very fact of our possessing those faculties proves that they were intended for use; & is it not by them that we should be guided, rather than by something revolting to them? And, besides, if this Bible was intended for the guidance of the human race, why was it not given to the whole race? The most of nations are destitute of this *blessing*. They have the faculties & yet no guidance. If it *was* intended as a guide to the world, it has, up to the present time at least,

32. Sir Walter Scott (1771–1832) was a Scottish novelist, poet, and playwright.
33. These issues of the *New York Mercury* do not appear to have survived.

miserably failed in its object, in that a comparatively small portion of that world has ever enjoyed its benefits.

Again, why was the race not originally perfection? We all suppose God to be good & just. If so why was man degraded to a position which necessitated a book of rule & guidance, when, by a mere exercise of the Creators will, all might have been perfect joy & bliss? "Why curse a race in order to necessitate a savior"?[34] Darwin tells us, "The long ascending line from dead matter to man, has been a progress Godwards: & the next step will unite Creator & creation in our person."[35] We *know* that the world has been a progress. Every age has stamped its predecessor as superstitious. Is it not fair to presume that ours will receive such treatment from the next? If progress has been steady, is it a justifiable supposition that we are the "ne plus ultra"?[36]

Such thoughts as these almost make me an Atheist. I am almost ready to subscribe myself to the sentiments, "I have no faith. I know that I exist & that a beautiful universe surrounds me. I am conscious of a multitude of conflicting emotions. Farther than this I dare believe nothing. I stand on the everlasting basis of all skepticism. 'There is no criterion in truth. All must be but subjectively, relatively true."[37] You say, "unhappiness is the result of man's willful & foolish actions; & not the consequence of any fault in his nature." I hold that the nature which will permit & even lead on to those actions is, of necessity, faulty. As we are, we were created. We had no volition in the matter, & I dont think we are responsible. On this ground, at least, I feel firm; & I assure you, you would be mistaken if you were to guarantee that my mind has not, in the last year, lingered for ten minutes on what will be my feelings when I come to my death struggle. I *have* thought of it; & feel safe, as I know my irresponsibility, whatever the eternal truth may be. If I were asked what else I believed, I would be tempted to answer; Nothing! If what I doubted? Nothing. My mind tells me that I have no inclination to worship. I look around & see all nations worshiping. I know not whether there be a God, or all things are ordered by chance. Some things in the world go fearfully wrong. Even everything pleasant is followed by something sad. Ike Marvel says, "Ashes follow blaze, as inevitably, as Death follows Life; Misery treads on the

---

34. This quotation comes from Evans, *Beulah,* 255.

35. Charles Darwin (1809–82) was an English biologist and naturalist whose most famous work, *On the Origin of Species* (1859), proposed a theory of evolution based on natural selection. This line, however, which is not an exact quotation, actually comes from Scottish geologist Hugh Miller's 1857 work, *The Testimony of the Rocks.*

36. A Latin phrase describing the "highest point capable of being attained."

37. This quotation comes from Evans, *Beulah,* 322.

heels of Joy: Anguish rides swift after pleasure."[38] If we have so much misery in this world, & then nine-tenths of our race suffer to all eternity after death, I can only think of God as cruel, vindictive, & possessed of all the evil qualities which I can imagine. If I had such a beliefe I would sooner be a dog than a human being. I am almost afraid to think of it, for with me, such thoughts *must* find expression.

When I think of how often I would write to you if I only owed you a letter, I feel as if I would like it better were we to drop all formality & write just when we feel inclined; without reference to answered or unanswered letters. Would such a correspondence suit you? Speaking of letters, dont you think the beginning of Ike Marvel's "Reveries by a city grate," is very near the truth? "They are the only true heart talkers."[39] But the reading of *this* letter, if I make it much longer, will bother you, & take more of your time than you have to devote to such subjects.

Your Friend,

Sing Ashenfelter

P.S. I have put so much in this that I have been unable to give it any arrangement; whatever you cant understand, pass by as valueless, & there, perhaps, you can go through it all, without being bored.

Idem[40]

---

38. This quotation comes from Marvel, *Reveries of a Bachelor,* 36.
39. Marvel, *Reveries of a Bachelor,* 53.
40. Latin for "the same."

CHAPTER THREE

1864

In the Room, alone,
Jan. 12th. 1864.

Dear Sam,

A short time since, you remarked, "We would not feel so much tenderness for this room, if it was destitute of the old crowd." I did not think so at that time:—I had imagined that I loved this place for itself alone. I wish I could tell you how deeply I feel, at the present moment, the truth of what you said.

Your Friend,

Sing Ashenfelter

I have just read, "'Léternité est une pendule, dont le balancier dit et redit sans cesse ces deux mots seulement, dans le silence des tombeaux: 'Toujours! jamais! Jamais! toujours!'"[1]

Idem

Ike[2] was just in the [YMLU] room & I delivered into his charge your skates, which had been left in the room.

Sing

1. This line in French—which translates, "Eternity is a clock, whose pendulum endlessly repeats the time in two words, amid the silence of tombstones: 'Forever (always)! never! never! forever (always)!'"—was originally written by the French Roman Catholic priest Jacques Bridaine. It was popularized in America as an epigraph to Longfellow's poem "The Old Clock on the Stairs" (1845).

2. Isaac R. Pennypacker (1852–1935) was SWP's younger brother. He grew up to become a noted journalist and historian. He edited SWP's *Autobiography* after his brother's death.

Dick. Coll.
February 16th, 1864

Dear Sam,

This is not a letter; but you shall have one, just as soon as I can find time to write it.

Excuse my delay.

　Your Friend

　Sing Ashenfelter

Dickinson College
Feb. 29th, 1864.

Dear Sam,

I have just reread yours of the 12th. ult. & if I believed in a conscience I would pronounce myself stricken therewith. I acknowledge that my delay is shameful & have determined to be silent no longer. Do not suppose that I offer this as a reply to yours of the 14th of Dec. It is merely a note promissory, explanatory;

Fig. 15. Class of 1865 outside of West College, ca. 1864. Ashenfelter is second from the left in the front row. (Courtesy of Archives and Special Collections, Dickinson College, Carlisle, PA)

& apologetic; In other words I apologize for my delay, explain it by stating that I had not sufficient time at command to write a reply worthy of your letter; & promise that you shall not have reason to complain in the future. I wish you to understand from this, firstly, That I am still in the land of the living; &, Secondly that my best friend is not forgotten. My thoughts this afternoon have no regularity & so you must not expect to find much order herein. I am writing—as I always do, to you—just what I think, & I am thinking just what I please. Following inclination therefore, & scribbling just what floats upon the surface of my mind—being most conveniently get-at-able—I do not anticipate that you will stumble upon the discovery of any great indication of depth of thought [or] elegence of expression.

You once asked me whether I ever experienced that devilish—I only use it as an adjective—feeling which, for the moment, tempted one to the commission of any deed. I felt so to-day & towards an apparently inoffensive, but cursed oily looking Freshman. I met him in the campus &, under the influence of that momentary inclination could have killed him on the spot.

I do not suppose it will surprise you to know that Annie & I correspond. I would give considerable to know whether or not I love her. I am so much of a hypocrite, though, that positive knowledge would make no difference in regard to my actions. Opposition to Dave Euen would be a sufficient incentive. I will reply to your letter just as soon as possible.

Your Friend

Sing Ashenfelter

P.S. You may, if you wish, regard this as another installment.

Idem

Dickinson College

Mar. 19th, 1864

At the eleventh hour, dear Sam, I sit down to reply to your's of the thirteenth of December. I suppose it is hardly necessary for me to review the causes of my delay. In fact, I believe they are already in your possession; & so, dropping all heartless & unmeaning apologies, I will proceed immediately to say my say.

The *page* which you devoted to the consideration of my remarks upon your correspondence with—well, with miss Alice Lee,[3] was no less amusing than in-

3. According to the 1860 census, Alice Lee, age twenty-one, lived near Phoenixville. From this and subsequent letters, she appears to have been a romantic interest of SWP's, although SWP does not appear to have preserved her correspondence. Lee may be the "certain young lady" SMA refers to on Nov. 22, 1863.

Fig. 16. Alice Lee. (Courtesy of
Pennypacker Mills, County of
Montgomery, Schwenksville,
PA)

teresting. How delightfully you circled about the real point of interest! How innocently expressed was that dullness of comprehension! How apparently eager
your desire for a full & explicit explanation of my meaning! How significant that
concluding "'Pon my word, Sing, I thought you knew me better!" The evident
necessity of association between the two sexes of our race has attracted my attention since I first began to think: & the curious manner in which particular traits
of character & peculiarities of nature in the one, exercise an attractive influence
upon certain individuals of the other, has been one of my most interesting studies. That you should be so influenced I had never anticipated. And the surprise
which my first information on the subject aroused was all the greater because un-
expected. I could not doubt the reliability of that information, because the source
from which it emanated was such as to render the facts fixed. I could only wonder
that the one whome I had imagined to be in the least danger from Cupid's darts,
should be among the first of those stricken. I fell to moralizing upon the subject,
& with such an example before me, could not but conclude that, sooner or later,
we must all worship our "bright particular." I presume that those delightful boat-
rides of last summer occasioned the birth & early development of this instance of

the tender passion—for so I suppose it must be called—& further, that you dwell upon certain romantic retrospections, & the remembrance of numerous trivial but significant incidents, with the most tender feelings imaginable.

Well, Sam, I pity you in the present, almost as much as I do myself of the past. I *believe* I am no longer in love; & as I look back & view the remarkable foolishness with which my actions were characterized, while the subtile sentiment still held & exercised its influence, I cannot but feel an amused sort of pity for the Ego that was.

Dont think me fickle or decei[t]ful; for whatever sentiments have been expressed to you were fully & deeply felt at the time; & the only difficulty is that nature has taken its course, & I have, partly at least, outgrown them. This is my feeling now, but strange to say, I am not positive as regards its continuance, when I am once fairly put to the test. Perhaps personal association will make me as foolish as ever, & the now smoldering fire will spring into new life under the genial influences of next summer vacation.

After this lengthy acknowledgement of apparent frivolity, you will doubtless wonder why I continue in correspondence with Annie. Well, I am supremely selfish—your opinion to the contrary notwithstanding—& seriously regard my future enjoyment. Being doubtful as to my real feelings, I look forward to any possibility. Almost, I would be heartless to correspond enough through mere opposition to my friend David, &—Pshaw! I believe I love her, after all. Let next summer decide. So ends this subject.

There was something in your letter for which I thank you. "I have felt for years as if there were more congeniality in our dispositions, as if I had more in common with you than any other of my friends." Those few words, standing there over your signature, are worth more to me than would be the high opinion of all others. From the bottom of my heart, I reciprocate your sentiment. I remember how, years ago, you made your first impression upon my mind. It was one evening, when I met you on your return from school. I had announced to someone an intention of numbering myself among Bradley's students. That evening, you asked me at what time I expected to commence my attendance at Grovemont.[4] The question, although in itself comparatively trivial, was asked in a manner which, to me, indicated a certain degree of interest. I dont know whether you remember the circumstance, but it made an impression upon my mind which can never be effaced. I almost feel as though I were writing foolishness, & if this was

---

4. Rev. Joel E. Bradley, whom SWP later recalled in his *Autobiography* as "a man of extensive acquirements," was a Baptist preacher who founded the Grovemont Seminary in Phoenixville. Both SMA and SWP attended the seminary.

for any one else, it most assuredly would not be forwarded. But I mean so fully what I say, & am moreover so confident that you will not misunderstand me, that I have no hesitation whatever in revealing even my most private thoughts. You know me too well to think me a flatterer when I tell you that I could open up to you the most secret chambers of my heart. In short you are the only person living, who, with my consent, may know Sing Ashenfelter as well as I do.

I cannot sympathize with Dick & Irvin,[5] but with Andy, to a certain extent, I can. My feelings toward him are those of a true friend. I like him very much, &, if in my power, would sacrifice considerable to aid him, should he need it. Lloyd has been my inigma. I would have hesitated, some months ago, to acknowledge that he puzzled me so much; for I more than half expected that you had un-ravelled him. I did not like to admit my inferior knowledge of human nature. I cannot comprehend him. Apparently he is wrapped up in a cloak of indifference to externals; & yet I know that he does not allow the most trivial circumstances to pass unnoticed; & frequently they exert a powerful influence over his actions. Sometimes he has a superabundance of animal spirits, & at others is as [illegible] as a mouse:—& it usually takes *me* about a half hour to ascertain what mood predominates. He will take up an idea & work it out to its fullest extent. This is why he visits Lide Vanderslice so frequently. All on account of an idea. He rea-sons to himself. People who do not know me at all think I am in love with her[.] People who know me in part, & those who know me best, do not understand this more, & it fills them with wonder. I rather enjoy the knowledge that I arouse such feelings in others, while I can laugh in my sleeve with a full understanding of my own motives. Besides all this I wish to show how utterly indifferent I am to outside remarks. He knows that his feelings are in no danger of becoming inter-ested; & that Lide is too frivolous to be earnestly & honestly in love, even if she wished so to be. And so while apparently indifferent to the opinions of others in the matter, those opinions in reality form his motive. I broke out with consider-able abruptness one evening last vacation & told him that this was the case, & at the same time laughed at him for his folly. He looked at me for some time in silence. At last, breaking into a light laugh, he made this remark. "Well, I guess you have pretty nearly hit the truth." After that, he was more open & confidential than ever I knew him to be before.

It is sometimes a source of considerable satisfaction to know that one is over-rated. As far as regards the world at large, I myself am desirous of standing in

5. Irvin J. Brower (1846–1907), a childhood friend and member of the Young Men's Liter-ary Union, worked at David Euen's drugstore. Later he became a businessman and president of the Phoenix Gas and Electric Company.

Fig. 17. Mary Eliza "Lide" Vanderslice. (Courtesy of Penny-packer Mills, County of Mont-gomery, Schwenksville, PA)

the highest possible estimation—with you I wish to be just what I am. It was this latter feeling, which induced me to tell you of my ambitious views, & of what I would sacrifice for their advancement. You say "The man who deliberately de-termines, as a rule for action through life, to sacrifice principle to his plans for advancement, must be a cold blooded calculating creature, which you are not & could not be if you would[.]" When I wrote those sentences which occasioned your remark, I intensely felt what I was writing. *I will not take a criterion of right, except it exist within myself.* What the world calls principle, I hold in utter con-tempt. If I see those around me striving for supremacy; if my mind points me to a good—I mean it—& glorious object; yes, even if what is termed hypocrisy & treachery are necessary to the attainment of my aim, I allow no popular idea of justice or right to deter me:—for I acknowledge none. By my own judgement alone will I be guided; & I recognize no evil in a false face or a politic action, so long as I injure thereby, nothing beyond what the world calls my moral nature. I would regard myself as doing a great wrong, were I to allow the prevalent stan-dard of morality to deter me from advancing my own interests. As I have said, *my* standard of right lies wholly solely & entirely within myself. I acknowledge the existence of that inner intuitive judgement,—it was the conscience from the "*Holy Ghost*"[6] that my last refered to—& I believe I can say truthfully that I seldom swerve from what it dictates. This may seem to you to be a very queer code of morality, but such as it is, it is mine. I can as frequently see right beneath a surface of wrong as wrong beneath a surface of right.

You & I differ as regards Henry Clay[7] & Chas. Sumner.[8] I would give an infinite preference to the name & position of the former. You ask me for my idea of ambition. It is essentially the same as your own; but differs in this particular—I care not for being known after death. When it ceases to give gratification I am willing to relinquish it. My reasons for this disregard of the future, I will give you hereafter. In my opinion your idea is remarkably well expressed. "To rule would be nothing—to be considered able to rule, as having ruled well, everything." The knowledge of power would give gratification; the knowledge of worth would brighten the gratification by the additional feeling of self approval. In all this, though, I am afraid that self is the supreme object:—& I may add, not only in this, but in all else. Does not everyone aim for happiness. Are not all our actions but stepping stones upon which we are crossing the stream of life & advancing towards what we imagine to be the highest point of our existence? No man ever does good unselfishly. We may give credit for purity of motive, but we do so unthinkingly.

Suppose we attempt to analyze the motives which prompt us to what is termed unselfishness. Making the application general, & reassuming our original basis;—that happiness, either in this world or the next is a universal aim,—what inference can we draw but that all our actions are directed to ultimate personal benefit—that selfishness ever predominates? What is sympathy? We see a fellow being in pain. Through our *knowledge* of what he suffers, certain emotions are aroused within us, & we are enabled to sympathize. If we were ignorant of what would be our own feelings under similar circumstances, *lack* of knowledge would destroy *ability* to sympathize. And so, on the supposition of *ego* being so affected, our feelings apply rather to ourselves, than to the apparent recipient. Immediate or ultimate personal enjoyment is a universal aim, & anything which tends to retard us in our progress thereto is regarded with fear & dislike. The existence of inherent selfishness is strikingly shown in this emotion of fear. We

6. "Holy Ghost" is underlined five times.

7. Henry Clay (1777–1852), a Kentucky slaveowner who served for many years as a Whig in the Senate, was known for his efforts at sectional compromise during the antebellum period.

8. Charles Sumner (1811–74), an abolitionist and Radical Republican senator from Massachusetts, was famously beaten with a cane on the floor of the Senate in 1856.

know of something which is liable to exercise a deleterious influence upon our person. Our natural distaste for anything unpleasant spurs us to the avoidance of that something[.] When doubt arises as to our ability in this respect,—when the subject matter is beyond the sphere of *ego*,—that is, above the comprehension of self—we experience the emotion of fear.

Suppose we view this in its religious application. The popular interpretation of the Bible makes fear the bulwark of Christianity. Men become attachees of the church of Christ not through intuitive inclination,—as justice would demand were Christianity of a God—or through love of their Creator, but merely through a fear of that Creator's vengeance. They dread the unknown, the untried future. Incapable of relying upon that self whose interests they are so desirous of advancing, they go out in search of something which will preserve them from so great ill as they imagine threatens them. The only inference then that we can draw is that Christianity is conceived in selfishness & supported by fear. We have morality though, have we not? In truth we have; but dare we scrutinize it? Morality, without Christianity is merely action dictated by love of self-approval. We are moral, not because we anticipate a reward or dread a punishment, but simply because we thereby enjoy a pleasant—a self congratulatory feeling. Then this too is dictated by selfishness? What is not? All love, all pity, all sympathy, is founded upon this miserable feeling—the predominance of the *ego*. Sometimes, Sam, I am disgusted with humanity, & myself as a part of it; but a thought of you will make me question whether selfishness even does not contain an element of merit. I perceive, however, that I have bored you long enough with this topic, & have, moreover, run out into the consideration of something foreign to the subject.

In my opinion, you underrate yourself when you say that the fact of a literary field of action requiring mental ability, talents, &c., is sufficient to deter you from entering thereon. You know, or at least I do, that the most of your acquaintances & friends regard you as something of a genius: & I think, in this case, the common opinion is pretty nearly right. In my opinion you *do* possess ability & talents, & I feel confident that if any considerations *ought* to influence the actions of a man, the ones you have named should induce you to enter upon literary life, with one doubt as to the result. Remember that I do not flatter, but write honestly. In my opinion, failure or inferiority is impossible to you in whatever sphere you might cho[o]se to exert yourself.

I could never content myself in that "far off island" even "with such a woman to love as my imagination often depicts." Nothing but the most abject wretchedness could accompany an existence so utterly devoid of all that renders life endurable. No ambition, no strife for supremacy, no feeling of superiority: none of the excitement of every day life, none of the strange enjoyment which one experiences when merged within the great crowd: nothing but a blank soulless existence, with each day the duplicate of the former, & with every idea & noble aspiration crushed beneath the terrible knowledge of sameness. Why, Sam, the sweets of the purest kind of love could not endure. They would pall through continuance. No! No! My weary head shall *never* rest upon that "fair maiden's breast." My purpose is too deeply settled, & my path through life too firmly fixed to allow the fascinations of even idealized beauty to induce me to swerve. Love & every other emotion must acknowledge itself inferior to the will which is inspired by ambition. Do not think me egotistical in this, for I write it as though I were "thinking to myself"—, & you know one may *think* according to inclination.

I was very much struck by the candor displayed in your description of Saml. In some points I think you hardly did justice to his character. When you say "*selfishness* is so prominent that I had almost forgotten it," I am tempted to attack my own theory upon that subject. I presume it is hardly necessary for me to lay my character open to your inspection, as you *know* me already. Better perhaps, than I know myself.

Speaking of myself reminds me of the fact that I made a speech sometime since. That is, I took my position upon the stage, & repeated from memory certain words, so arranged as to indicate very little meaning, & a great deal of high sounding bombast; & which were, moreover, as far as the individual speaking was concerned, a collection of most miserable lies. I took Perfection for my theme, endeavored to prove that it was a universal intuitive conception—that it could not exist in this life because it involved the idea of eternal continuity, & would, moreover, admit of no such thing as unhappiness—& that, consequently, the future beyond death was the field of its operation. I wrote it because of duty, delivered it for effect, & destroyed it through disgust. I was very highly congratulated upon it, &, instead of feeling grateful, pitied any one who could be so foolish as to imagine it of any worth. I did not feel in the least degree embarrassed when I took my position upon the stage. In fact my feelings were rather those of antagonism to the audience than anything else. I felt that they came there with their sober long-drawn faces, &, submitting to be bored with speeches containing nothing but highsounding phrazes, & meaningless murmuring, went home with their minds made up as to the respective merits or demerits of those who had acted the hypocrite, for the special purpose of creating an impression[.] Oh! The depth, the profundity of these College speeches. The tremendous displays of oratory by which their delivery is accompanied. The orators of the past would stand aghast were they to hear the reverberating tones which swell up from the youth of the present. Custom dictates the attempt at sobriety, but it appears to me to be cursed folly to take a poor swimmer beyond his depth. Sometimes I get terribly blue. I am disgusted with everything. I can do nothing but sit & think of the *dark* phazes of human existence. At such moments, my feelings approximate those of the suicide. I feel now,—for I am under the miserable influence— as though I would almost willingly exchange the present life for nonexistence, could I do so without pain. Were it not for those who might regret my death, I could easily reconcile myself to the end. It may seem strange that one in a bodily condition so healthy as mine should talk upon this subject, but low spirits almost make me curse the hour I was born.

My mood has changed since I wrote the above, & with it I will change the subject. I have often wondered how you, who, as I imagine, have a feeling of contempt for Royer & his tribe, could become a contributor to the *Phoenix*.[9] In other words, how you could *quibble*. I cannot think that you are especially desirous of securing the high opinions of the people of Phoenixville, because I do not think you care for them. In fact I am at a loss to account for your condesencion—for it is nothing else—unless you are carrying out one of your queer ideas.

I write this while sitting upon the College steps, & the beauty of the surrounding scenery is almost sufficient to make me poetic. To tell the truth, I am almost tempted to branch out into sentiment, but am restrained because past experience has taught me the folly of such an attempt. "I have no poetry in my soul"; or at least, if I have it *there* it does not extend to my finger ends. I have not attempted anything in that line for a long time past & will not for a long time to come. I am, however, indebted to my power of rhyming for its past services. When I came to Dickinson I arose into some consideration on account of a few parodies, written at that time, & posted anonymously upon the bulletin board. They held the President of [the] College up to ridicule, & of course took well among the students. The individual who was, at that time, my roommate [Charles W. Bickley], knew of my having written them, &, as he could not keep quiet, the knowledge soon spread among the students. The other day, in looking over some old papers, I found the original copies of those effusions. I read them & threw them into the fire, almost swearing that I would never rhyme again.

You stated, I think, in your letter, that you attended church regularly. I suppose you are aware that I do not attend at all. I believe I never told you my *reasons,* for what seems to be merely the result of indifference. Well my *conscience* will not permit me to enter a building devoted to worship. It will not permit me to take particular pains to become a regular listener to what I do not believe. For,

9. John Royer, age sixty-seven in the 1860 census, was a printer in Phoenixville who published the *Independent Phoenix,* a newspaper that ran from 1857 to 1879. In 1876 Vosburg Shaffer became publisher of the paper.

by an attendance at church, I tacitly or at least apparently admit the truth of what is there advanced. That is I periodically act the hypocrite. In this case, I do not see sufficient personal benefit for justification, & so I recognize a wrong. I quote from you as follows. "A man stands upon the verge of a precipice, with perfect power to throw himself over, or to turn about & go safely away—he chooses the former & dashes himself to pieces, who is responsible"? Let us in the first place view this in the light of the existence of a God. The last motive which that man felt was the one which induced him to destroy himself. This was, then, the immediate cause. But this cause must have originated somewhere: something certainly induced its existence. That is, relatively to something antecedent it must have existed as an effect. But that cause antecedent must also have been a relative effect: & so on, *ad infinitum.* Thus we go from the individual through his ancestors, back to the origin of the race. Now I claim, viewing it in this light, that the Creator was the first great cause, & that consequently the responsibility lies with him. Not the responsibility of this alone, but of every evil deed committed upon earth. With a creator man is totally irresponsible. Now, suppose we view it merely as a personal matter. This man's existence is his own. He has within him no natural feeling of accountability. He knows that he exists, but knows not wherefor. He knows also that existence is burdensome. Now, whenever a man can see nothing but misery before him, & feels certain that the brief pain of ending being contains more of pleasure—for it has a negative element—and less of pain than the endurance required by existence;—at that moment, death becomes pleasant, & we are justified in seeking it. As we live for enjoyment, I here recognize no responsibility whatever. The man has simply shown that he prefers death to life, &—to use a common phraze—it's nobody's business.

"To impugn the actions of God is useless & presumptuous folly." What would you say to denying, or at least refusing to admit the existence of a God. At that point I have finally arrived. I began by doubting the justice of eternal punishment. Then, I was but little more than a child. But though a child, my whole nature rebelled against the idea of being created, so to suffer. I had been taught a firm belief in the Bible, &, not daring to doubt, vainly endeavored to reconcile ultimate universal redemption with its teachings. I say vainly, because I could not view the matter in any other light than that of reason. As I grew older, & my faculties became more fully developed, the struggle became more intense. My early teachings made me reverence the Bible & doubt or disbelief seemed fearful. Reason, on the other hand, showed me that while endless punishment was terribly unjust, & consequently could not be of God, the Bible, assuming to be the revealed word of that God, nevertheless, advanced & supported it. Here was a plain contradiction. I was in a dilemma & had to choose. Hard as it was to abandon the old impressions, I clung to reason, & doubted the truth of the scriptures. Up to this time I had never read one argument against christianity. All had sprung, as it were, from intuition. Having once decided that the scriptures were unworthy of belief, I immediately began to speculate. I read eagerly whatever bore any relation to the subject & finally came to the conclusion that we were warrented in believing in nothing but a God. That every thing moved according to his will, & consequently all that the future held in store was ordered. With this belief I felt confident of man's irresponsibility. I did not rest satisfied here, but continued to speculate. I once read "Le bon Dieu[10] created the mouse. He said I have done a bad thing. So, he created the cat. The cat is the erratum of the mouse. The cat plus the mouse is a perfect creation."[11] It set me to thinking. You can imagine what followed, then. I saw creation at war with itself. I saw like struggling with like & unlike. I saw in the highest types of being all that I knew of evil, all of wretchedness. And I believed in a God no longer. With this faith fell my hope for the future. I asked myself,—does not the idea of immortality necessitate that of a previous existence? Can we believe that our being has no end unless we feel assured that it had no beginning? Nothing tells me of a past life, & consequently I cannot believe in a future one. Like all other animals we come upon the world in youth, draw a certain number of breaths during life, & are merged into dust after death. I am an utter skeptic in all things.

　　Your Friend

　　Sing Ashenfelter

P.S. I do not think your last picture as good as the first one. When you reply tell me of the article of one hundred pages of foolscap.

Idem.

　　　　　　　　　　　　　　　　　　　　　　　Dickinson College

　　　　　　　　　　　　　　　　　　　　　　　　　May. 1864

Dear Sam,

　　Since sunset, I have been laying upon the grass, thinking. Recalling what has been & surmising the *will-be*. Down there, among the spring buds, an intense longing came over me—A longing for sympathy. I felt as though I were almost entirely adrift. No hope in the future; no enjoyment in the present. All, blank, blank being. The day has been a holiday, & I have spent it in musing on the infinite. Out there, in an imaginary realm, I was nearer, I thought, to a sympathetic

10. French for "The good Lord."

11. SMA here paraphrases Victor Hugo's *Les Miserables* (1862), bk. 1, chap. 2.

heart. Oh, how I long for—I know not what. A something in common with my-self. A present friend[.]

Dear Sam, I wish I could find words to express my intense loneliness. I am not homesick, but friendsick. Lying out there, beneath the clear sky, I felt as though I would have given worlds for one of your old familliar tones. Did you ever feel a pity, a half loving pity for humanity? That feeling was with me as I thought. I felt a love of the universe. I believe I could have embraced a serpent. And why not? The idea is neither new nor "strange to me.["] If they are faulty, it is not of themselves. One of Lamertine's[12] characters loved the very clods of the earth. The world's great heart, he said, beat in unison with his own. There, in the dust, lay the germ of future being. Why despise it, because undeveloped. Do not let this scriblling of thoughts make you wonder. From out [of] my mood, a desire to hear you rose supreme. If I had had the will, I could not have refrained from writing.

Your Friend,

Sing Ashenfelter

Dickinson

June 5th /64

Dear Sam,

I have not time to write a letter, & so, I "drop a line[.]"

The enclosed will explain itself.[13] I would be very happy to see you in Carlisle.

Your Friend

Sing Ashenfelter

P.S. I wrote the above signature [it is sloppy] while glancing at a fellow student; I forward it as an addition to your collection

Idem

Dickinson College

June 11th, 1864

Dear Sam,

For some time I have been laboring under the awkward consciousness of a

---

12. Alphonse de Lamartine (1790–1869) was a French poet, historian, and politician. The character referred to here is Claude from *The Stonecutter of St. Point: A Village Tale* (London: George Rutledge, 1851), who said, "not one of these clods of earth turned over my spade to the sun, in my childhood; for which I do not feel a profound attachment" (58).

13. Whatever SMA enclosed is unknown.

duty unpreformed [unperformed]. To-night the twinges of "the inward monitor" were so painfully felt that I could endure no longer. Hence, this letter. You speak at some length, in your last, of my habit of swearing. Well, in the first place, I wish to assure you that it was entirely unnecessary for you to accompany what you said with any excuse for alluding to the subject. I hope you will never have any hesitation whatever in telling me of, & strongly censuring my faults. Many persons have received & most of persons would receive a direct insult for attempting to correct me in that respect; but any allusion to it coming from yourself or Lloyd could not but be received in the same spirit with which it was made. If you had the opportunity of double observation you would find that, in your presence, I swear less than in that of any other. I do not wish to attempt any justification of the habit; I acknowledge all that is said in condemnation:—but, I do think that you misinterpret the motive—or rather, the *lack* of motive. I do *not* swear because I am indifferent to the opinions of those about me; or because I wish to set those opinions at defiance. No such sentiments enter in. The whole truth of the matter is that I swear in opposition to my will, to what I know to be politic to what I know to be right, & to what I know to be sensible. Did you ever read Poe's "Imp of the Perverse["]?[14] If you did, you can understand me more fully. I do this because I do not wish to do it. Because I know it to be against my best interests,—& because I know I thereby act very foolishly. If there is any motive here, then I swear with some inducement. If not,—then I know not what. The whole thing is more unaccountable to me than it *can be* to any one else. For the first month of this session *I did not use one strong expression,* but for the last three I have more than made the account square. If anything *can* make me stop, your wishes will do it.

In regard to that *genius* business, I will say more at some future time; I will tell you though, that, since the time of the oft' referred to "lemon story," I have ceased flattering. But, you say, "Talents I may have &c." Can you tell me the difference between Talent & Genius? I would much like to know in what it consists. I hope soon to see Whitey's grave.[15]

Your Friend,

Sing Ashenfelter.

P.S. I assure you that the *reliable information* to which I alluded in my last, is of such a nature, & comes from such a source as will admit of no doubt. You have

14. Edgar Allan Poe's "The Imp of the Perverse" (1845) is a short story about acting against one's self-interest. In it "the imp of the perverse" induces people to commit acts they know to be self-destructive.

15. Josiah White (1834–64) was a childhood friend of SMA and SWP's who died as a Union soldier on May 18, 1864. For more on his life and death, see the introduction.

in no instance made a direct denial of the correspondence with that young lady in N.Y., & until you do so, I must believe in the existence of such correspondence. I cannot be convinced by any allusions to "Fudge, Nonsense &c. &c."

Idem

[*Editors' Note:* In the following letter Ashenfelter refers to his letter of May 14 but likely means the preceding letter of May 11.]

Dickinson College
June 19th, 1864

Dear Sam,

How could you, for a moment, suppose that I felt hurt at the remarks in yours of the 16th ult.? I surely did not intend to convey any such impression by mine of the 14th. I did not suppose that your allusion to swearing was dictated by a desire to correct, & even if I had, I cannot see that I would have been justified in feeling in any degree hurt or offended. On that point I certainly deserve correction. I do feel it though, that you should suppose it possible for me to take your remarks on any such subject in a spirit differing from that in which they were made. I have *almost* determined that you shall see that your allusion to the subject was not made in vain. I say *almost* because closing Spring will not admit of any thing more definite. In such weather as the present I cannot be decided upon anything.

Were you not surprised some time since, while on a visit to Phoenixville, at being taken into Lloyd's confidence as regards his frequent visits to Vanderslice's? I would have asked you the question in my last letter, had I not forgotten it. I ask it knowing what the answer will be. I heard of Lloyds adventures with the night-watches from Sister,[16] I think it an excellent joke. By the way, Sister wrote to me a month or so since requesting me to acknowledge for her the receipt of one of your *Cartes de Visite*,[17] & to return thanks for the same. She said that she did not know your directions. Please consider the thing as done.

If you write to me again this *month,* as I hope you will, tell me on what day you expect to arrive in Phoenix. I leave here on the 1st of July.

16. This reference likely refers to SMA's older sister, Hannah. He had another sister, Martha (1846–1911), and appears to have had a third sister who died as a child, Emma (born 1838). Martha went by "Emily" and appears as "Emmie" in the letter of April 24, 1865.

17. Cartes de visite are small paper photographs. They began to gain widespread market appeal in the late 1850s and were prevalent during the Civil War for the ease with which they could be given away or mailed.

Your Friend

Sing Ashenfelter

(over)

Evening, June 20th

After writing the above letter on Sunday evening I started out to walk for a few min. in the moonlight. Two of my fellow students were in company with me. We walked up the rail road to a distance from town of about half a mile. There, we threw ourselves upon the grass, & took to moongazing. Suddenly, some one proposed to walk all night. The others expressed themselves as willing. Off we started. The contents of my [Ashenfelter likely forgot to write a word here] were *one* key, *one* pipe, a little tobacco, & three matches. I was with out colar. My total attire being one linen coat, one shirt, boots, stockings & pants & hat. The other two the same, except the poet, Jackson, (who formed one of the trio) who instead of boots had only slippers. During the night we walked twenty miles. We have just returned pretty tired. I will give you a full account at some future time[.]

[Y.M.L.U] Reading Room

July 19th. [1864] 2 A.M.

Dear Sam,

Here it is, two o'clock Tuesday morning, & the meeting which assembled at eight last night is treating itself to a recess of one hour. We have been having a gay old time of it. Lloyd has just interrupted me with a request to "give my respects to Pennie & tell him that 'my bosom swells' & that I'm all right." He occupies a chair near the settee & is reared back for a comfortable snooze. Andy is giving me extracts from the minutes as I jot them down.

"Up to eleven & fifteen minutes fines amount to six cents. Two motions for adjournment lost. 12:15 fines twelve cents. 12:35, Recess of 15 min. 12:50, fines 26 cents. Recess for one hour. (2 o'clock, Recess for one hour) &c of[f] & on until adjournment[.] Approved A. R. Whitaker[."]

Well, Shaffer has all of his recruits & they thought they could keep us here until we were tired out. But we will be d—d if we dont see who caves first. (Lloyd growls out "my bosom swells[.]") Morgan[18] is stretched out on the settee vainly endeavoring to catch a short nap. Shaffer—d—n him stretched out on the sofa. His crowd are out taking a walk. Tom[19] has just ejaculated "do you hear the chickens crowing?"

18. We have been unable to identify Morgan.
19. We have been unable to identify Tom.

During the recess of the first hour, we went up to Euens drug store to rout Irvin.[20] Lloyd put on my coat & Andy's hat, tied a handkerchief over his face, & went up to ring the door bell. Mrs. Euen[21] came to the window & asked what was wanted. "Prescription" was the reply[.] "Who is it," was asked, "Mr. Jones" answers Lloyd. The window is closed & we skedaddle. Irvin wont cuss when he discovers himself to be a sold youth. Lloyd has just taken an easier position, with the remark "I'm Mr. Jones[.]" As the meeting progresses I will report.

Andy incloses a sketch of Lloyd. Later[.] Hurrah! Three Cheers. Three o'clock & shaffer not on hand. Bully for us. Ashen, Mellon, & Andy fined one cent for playing cards. Sundry fines, among which Shaffer ten cents for absence.

"Four o'clock—fines amount to 98 cents.["] We will keep it up until morning now.

Your Friends
Sing Ashenfelter
Andw R Whitaker
H. Lloyd
Five o'clock

P.S. Lloyd says "three cheers for the swells"[22]

Adj. at six o'clock
We came out triumphant

P.S. I will write on more important matters in a day or two.[23]

20. Irvin J. Brower had significant responsibilities at David Euen's drugstore, but he once complained in 1864 that "the Drug business at present is very dull as there is not many sick people now." See Brower to SWP, Jan. 10, July 24, 1864, Apr. 23, 1865, PM.

21. Mary Ann Neal (1819–1900) married David Euen on February 26, 1845. She is listed in the 1880 census as living with Annie but apart from David, indicating that they may have been separated. Records at the Chester County Archives, however, reveal that the couple never divorced; they are buried together along with Annie.

22. According to J. Matthew Gallman, "swells" were foppish, "true young dandies who populated urban clubs and elite colleges, adopting exaggerated modes of dress and speech." See Gallman, *Defining Duty in the Civil War: Personal Choice, Popular Culture, and the Union Home Front* (Chapel Hill: Univ. of North Carolina Press, 2015), 35–46.

23. Two days later Irvin J. Brower wrote: "What do you think of the proceedings of the Young Men's Literary Union on Monday evening[?] I think the members present must have been very anxious to sit up[.] I think some of them must have had a hard time to keep awake as a few most likely was up late the night before." See Brower to SWP, July 21, 1864, PM.

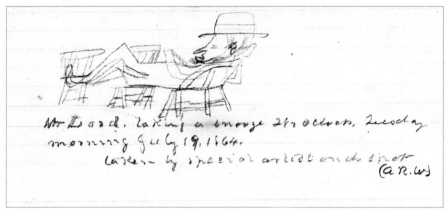

Fig. 18. Sketch of Horace Lloyd during a Young Men's Literary Union meeting, by A. R. Whitaker, appended to Ashenfelter's letter of July 19, 1864. (Courtesy of Pennypacker Mills, County of Montgomery, Schwenksville, PA)

Mr Lord, taking a snooze 2½ o clock, Tuesday morning July 19, 1864.

    taken by special artist on the spot

(A R.W)

[*Editors' Note:* A few months later Lloyd informed Pennypacker, "Sing had given you an erroneous impression in regard to my 'withdrawing to a certain extent the support I have heretofore given the Literary.'" Lloyd was "certainly disgusted with the way things go on there now, and only wish we had enough members to control those infernal cusses, but as to 'withdrawing,' never!" He considered removing some of his books "because the room is left open and all the windows [are] up nearly every night in the week, and somebody will go up there and help themselves if they find such invitations continually offered, and I am not particularly anxious to have mine stolen along with the rest." He also did not think his personal belongings there were being respected. Lloyd had been contributing his own copies of *Harper's Weekly* and had seen them "flying around the floor or in those dirty spittoons, with a good prospect of losing one half the numbers, so that when I want to bind it it will be in a pretty condition to do so." It was for these reasons that he considered taking his books and periodicals home. Yet Lloyd worried that doing this might "*seem* like spite work, or would have a tendency to render the shanty less attractive to those whom I count as my friends—I am afraid however that if things go on much longer as they have gone, the interest of some of the good members will be lost, and nothing remain but a lot of Shaffer's trash."

It appears that much of Lloyd's frustrations revolved around Vosburg Shaffer wanting to assume the presidency of the YMLU in the wake of Josiah White's death. "I suppose Shaffer will ride into the Presidency or Treasuryship with colors flying," he complained to Pennypacker. "They tried to put him in for Treasurer last time but did not quite come it, and I should not wonder if they would try it again if he does not get the Presidency." Lloyd further stated that he did "not want to hold the office particularly but I'll be darned if I want to see him have it." He declared indignantly, "Leave the Shanty for that contemptible cuss and his crew, no sir!" As it turned out, Pennypacker ended up winning election as president of the YMLU.[24]]

Phoenixville
July 21st. 1864

Dear Sam,

I commence, at last, a piece of work which has been resting upon my mind for over a week. The note which I scribbled on Monday night, or rather, Tuesday morning was not intended as a reply to yours of the 17th. inst., but was written simply to show you what d—d fools we are. Speaking of fools reminds me of the fact that lately I have shown myself to 'be' "the greatest fool among them all." It is a tedious story, but, trusting that you will not be *too* much bored I will relate it.

I had been endeavoring, ever since my return home, to obtain an interview with Annie; but my efforts were vain, until last Saturday. On that morning I discovered that she was in the habit of going, twice a week, into the country, to give music lessons. I dropped a note, offering to accompany her. The offer was accepted. I could not call at the house, & so we met on the road. She had said, in one of her letters, that *reasons* were given for the opposition to our intercourse. Those reasons I already suspected,—for, "a guilty conscience needs no accuser"[25]—but I wished to place the matter beyond doubt. So I asked her what the reasons were. After considerable hesitation she at last asked me whether I had not been intoxicated in Harrisburg while on my way home, & whether I had not spoken of the

24. Horace Lloyd to SWP, Sept. 4, 1864, PM; *Autobiography*, 73. Shaffer was elected president in December 1864. See Irvin J. Brower to SWP, Dec. 13, 1864, and Jan. 31, 1865, PM.

25. This phrase appears to have been a general axiom by the Civil War era. It appears in Samuel Maunder's book *Maunder's Treasury of Knowledge and Library of Reference* (London: Samuel Maunder, 1830) and is quoted in English grammar books of the time, such as Rev. Dr. Brewer's *A Guide to English Composition* (New York: C. S. Francis, 1854), 315.

Fig. 19. Anna J. Euen. (Courtesy of Pennypacker Mills, County of Montgomery, Schwenksville, PA)

same upon the Reading Room porch. I was surprised & astonished; but amazement predominated when she continued, "Have you not taken intoxicating drink, since your return, both over at Mont Clare[26] & in Oberholtzer's[27] drug store?" Now, all these things are true. I *did* speak on the porch of the few gay hours I had spent in Harrisburg, & I *had* drank at both places she mentioned. Do you see the *d—d* fool, now? I replied not one word. After a long silence she said, "Sing, if you deny all this, I will believe you." I had been debating whether I should attempt to deceive her, but those words of her's placed me beyond doubt. I kept silence until we drew near to her destination, & then I stopped her, & spoke somewhat as follows. "I am going to speak to you Annie, as I would to a sister. I think your duty is plain. Until you are perfectly satisfied that such accusations against me are false, you should have nothing further to do with me. My evidence could have no

26. In 1862 SWP taught at the one-room schoolhouse in Mont Clare, Pennsylvania.

27. Levi Oberholtzer (1832–1922), an 1854 graduate of the University of Pennsylvania School of Medicine, was a physician in Phoenixville who owned a drugstore in town. He was married to Angeline (or Angelina) Vanderslice, Lide's older sister.

weight, or at least should have none, & so I will neither acknowledge nor deny." (You saw the fool a bit ago; do you see the coward now?) So I bade her farewell & told her I should not feel hurt if she did not recognize me until she was satisfied. So the matter rested until Tuesday; then I wrote to her; for I could not bear the idea of deceiving *her* any longer. I wrote that her worst suspicions were more than verified by the reality:—that what I had said on Saturday was doubly applicable now;—that I could be nothing to her until I was something to myself. I wrote it & delivered it:—& then went down [the] street & took a big drink.—D—d fool, again.—

So that little matter is at an end. Unless I become a *reformed youth;* which is more improbable now than ever before. I find I have written until almost time for the mail to close & so, must defer replying to yours of the 17th. until—perhaps tomorrow.

Write when convenient.

Your Friend

Sing Ashenfelter.

Phoenixville
July 24th, 1864

Dear Sam,

I wrote to you a few days since but neglected at the time to reply to yours of last Sunday[.] I will endeavor to do so now.

I entirely agree with you when you say that, in ninety-nine cases out of a hundred, man wastes his energies in useless pursuits. This business of existence appears to me to be the most miserable humbug of all. We must all work. Every one has duties here upon earth which must be performed. And no matter how distasteful—no matter how injurious, even, to his neighbors, he who works & screws & twists, & toils into a *position,* even through mental & bodily prostration, has performed the labor of life—has discharged the responsibilities which devolved upon him through birth, & receives the applause of his co-workers in misery. Oh! this world & its affairs *are* beautifully ordered. Everything *does* move in perfect concord, & creation is a glorious success. No, Sam, I *am* one of those beings—contemptible though they be—who cannot admire creation as it is. Egotistical as it may seem, I will say that if I could not improve upon the present order of things, I would hurl that order out of being. Better no life at all than such as this. To tell the truth, I cannot look about me without seeing such faults in nature as would necessitate a contempt for a creator, could I persuade myself to believe in one. You may say that the fault is in myself, that all this disorder results from unnatural causes, &c; but that makes no difference in my impressions. And besides any fault in me is a fault of the nature of which I am a part. In going to war, man acts according to his nature, & if war is wrong, that nature must be faulty. If nature was so well ordered would there be any such thing as a long drought, pestilence, famine, the destruction occasioned by volcanos & earthquakes, &c. &c.? The more I think on the subject the more faults I can see; & I am even egotistical enough to believe that *I* could improve upon this present. But I suppose you think that this is all humbug; & I will change the subject.

As to the syllogisms. Does the fact that Descartes[28] holds certain opinions prove that those opinions are the correct ones? I do not suppose that you entertain such an idea, but your words certainly convey the impression that you would attach much weight to his opinions. Now I would not pretend to deny that Logic has had able & determined opponents. Among the number, I think, comes Spinoza.[29] I would not attach much weight to any man's opinion in metaphysics unless I could adopt it as my own. So you see a quotation from your author, while confirming your opinions, could not have the least weight upon mine.

I really think that the regular course of reasoning leads to the discovery of many important truths. We will take the case of Newton,[30] to which you alluded the other day. He laid the foundation for the discovery of the law of gravitation by a course of reasoning. The real process in his mind must have been—the apple falls—nothing can fall without a cause—therefor something caused the apple to fall. It may have been even impreceptable [imperceptible] to him, but first through such a sylogism must his mind have gone before he could be satisfied that something did occasion the fall; & this conclusion led to his discovery.

Examples are numerous but I suppose it would hardly be worth while to produce them. Small chance for conviction on either side, I guess.
(Page Sixth.)

I suppose you are becoming an idealist. I am nearer to materialism. I think that the truth is either *with* one of us, or between us. What say you? Someday, when I join "the elect," & have my name enrolled in the "lamb's book of life,"—a day far off, now—I shall expect to look back with holy horror upon the

28. Rene Descartes (1596–1650) was a French philosopher, scientist, and mathematician who became known as the father of modern philosophy and for his famous axiom, "I think; therefore I am."

29. Baruch Spinoza (1632–77) was a Dutch philosopher most famous for his work *Ethics* (1677).

30. English physicist and mathematician Sir Isaac Newton (1643-1727) is regarded as one of the most influential scientists in history.

opinions which I now hold.[31] I look forward to the life of a hypocrite, & a fine prospect it is. But with such prospects it does seem rather strange that I should put them upon paper. You see how completely I trust you.

Your Friend

Sing Ashenfelter

P.S. Your picture of the crowd was true in some respects, but false in others. Neither Lloyd nor Dick were present & for a wonder I was neither on the sofa, nor cursing the flies. Andy was not expected.

Idem.

Phoenixville

July 25th. 1864

Dear Sam,

Your letter was received this morning & I sit down with the intention of replying, & yet with no very definitively formed idea of what I am going to write. Your letter has set me to thinking, & as usual, thinking has given me the blues. Look whichever way I will, I am forever seeing myself acting the part of a fool[32] & indeed, I am almost persuaded that such in [is?] my actual character. No one knows better than myself how contemptible was the impulse which lead me to drink after I handed Annie that letter. It was not done with any idea of borrowing from the future. I did not wish "to shut out the darkness of the present.["]— If I had, other means would have been taken: for drinking could only bring it up more vividly—No, it was some mad impulse which urged me on to tempt all of [the] evil in my nature. I felt like flinging defiance in the face of Fate, &—made a fool[33] of myself.

As to drinking itself;—I have no apetite for liquor. I cannot even say that I like its effects. But some nameless sort of a feeling—& all the stronger for being indefinable—urges me on, & I never think of danger. A curious fascination, like that which I imagine one would feel while walking on the verge of a precipice. Entirely secure, & yet with the knowledge of life & death within grasp.

31. SMA here refers to the Calvinist doctrine of unconditional election, which espouses that God chooses those whom he will save. The "Lamb's Book of Life" refers to a list of those who believe in Jesus Christ and will be admitted to heaven.

32. SWP apparently did not like what SMA had written here. He drew a box around the word "fool" and wrote, "Expunged by S.W.P."

33. SWP again "expunged" this word.

I had determined, long since, that at the close of my College life I would cease drinking. Even my selfishness showed me the necessity of *that*. When I wrote I unthinkingly & yet at the time earnestly said that reformation was now farther off than ever. I believe I can take that back. Certainly I cannot entertain such an idea, having read your letter. I have concluded that this shall not affect my life. As I live, that original determination shall be carried out. *Not one drop shall pass my lips from the time I graduate until my dying day.*

Later.

"If friendship can add ought to the appeals of love, then *I conjure* you to stop now." What was impossible to *love, friendship* has accomplished. An hour's thought has decided. My eye caught the lines I quote, & I pushed the paper aside to think.

I will not touch any intoxicating drink again.

Your Friend,

Sing Ashenfelter

Phoenixville

August 5th. 1864

Dear Sam,

As I am tired of doing nothing, I drop you a few lines, just happening to be in the humor. I believe I forgot to answer an inquiry made in one of your late letters as to whether I knew whence Annie derived her information of my habits. I do not; & to me, that is the most misterious part of it. She entered so fully into the particulars that whoever told her, I am convinced, must have associated with myself. Beyond this I cannot satisfy my curiosity. Annie said she did not wish to tell, & I did not press the matter. I am extremely anxious for College to open, as my surroundings are not, at present, suggestive of the most pleasant trains of thought. Carlisle & a busy session are vastly preferable to P— & *ennui*.

Affairs political look a little blue. Grant's failure is not the sweetest pill in the world.[34] We are not much worse off than we were, but it is vexatious to think of what "might have been."

The hovering of the Rebels along the Potomac causes a devilish disagreeable

---

34. During the Overland Campaign in the spring of 1864, Lt. Gen. Ulysses S. Grant (1822–85) suffered an estimated 60,000 Union casualties. Despite this high number of losses, he kept pushing forward against the Confederate forces under Gen. Robert E. Lee (1807–70). Since mid-June the two generals had been locked in siege lines around Petersburg, Virginia, Grant seemingly stalemated from capturing Richmond and ending the Southern rebellion.

feeling, & withal I am somewhat bluishly inclined, & so a little item of agreeable news would be very acceptable. Cant Philadelphia start a favorable sensation rumor? Can you prove to me our *right* to whip the South,—our ability being admitted? I ask to ascertain what you really think.—local predjudice aside. I know a very intellectual young fellow—now a student in a German University—who hates the South & her institutions most intensely & yet is opposed to the war from principle. I simply ask to know your honest opinions, & I do not wish you to imagine I am other than I have been—a pro-war abolitionist. I feel as though the South should be made to understand that she cannot do just as she pleases.

But the evening mail will close soon & I must anticipate it at that business.

Your Friend

Sing Ashenfelter

[*Editors' Note:* While Pennypacker's response to Ashenfelter does not survive, some of his other surviving correspondence and writings reveal his views of the war.

Pennypacker was a lifelong Republican, from before the Civil War and through his career as governor of Pennsylvania in the early twentieth century. In February 1861, when President-elect Lincoln stopped at Independence Hall to raise a flag, Pennypacker and his grandfather went into Philadelphia to watch the ceremonies. He wrote the following day: "We saw him make a speech and afterward at our request (I mean the crowd's) the lesser celebrities quit the stand and almost left him alone in his glory. He took off his coat and hat, seized the rope, and the flag ran up to the top of the State House very easily and prettily without any hesitation or accident to make the omen a bad one." Pennypacker observed: "Rumor said that Lincoln was a horribly ugly man and rumor never told a greater falsehood—he is quite a good looking man with some resemblance to his photographs but very little. He has dark hair & whiskers. I believe every one who saw him was favorably impressed with him, and we made our way out of the crowd with high hopes and expectations and doubtless feeling very patriotic." After Lincoln raised the flag, Pennypacker's grandfather turned to him and said, "I think he will do."[35]

At the beginning of the war, Pennypacker exhibited "strong confidence" in Union general and Radical Republican John C. Frémont.[36] Although he never

---

35. SWP to Uncle, Feb. 23, 1861, Historical Society of Pennsylvania, Philadelphia; *Autobiography*, 83.

36. John C. Frémont (1813–90) had been an explorer in California during the late 1840s and in 1856 was the first Republican candidate for president. During the Civil War, he served

enlisted in a three-year regiment, Pennypacker spent "six weeks in uniform" as a member of the 26th Pennsylvania Emergency Militia during the Confederate invasion of Pennsylvania in the summer of 1863.[37]

Throughout the war, Pennypacker exuded disdain and derision for antiwar Democrats, or Copperheads. During the Pennsylvania gubernatorial election of 1863, he returned to Independence Hall, this time to watch a "Copperhead meeting." He "listened to the spoutings of a few of their second rate orators upon the anniversary of the adoption of that 'Constitution' for which they now profess such unbounded love and admiration. There was a large collection of patriots present with oil lamps and numerous transparencies, while the representations of the 'dimmycratic party' exhibited their contempt for 'ould Abe' and their determination to uphold the principles of constitutional liberty and freedom of speech by continuous shoutings, clappings, and hurrahings the vigor of which sundry potations of whiskey materially increased. In fact about the best point I heard made, and the one which received the greatest applause, was that in a few years, if the war continued and taxes increased, the price of whiskey would be raised so high that none but shoddy contractors would be able to buy it."[38] When Union general George B. McClellan came out in favor of the Democratic nominee for governor in Pennsylvania a few weeks later, Pennypacker concluded, "I think the estimate I formed of that nincompoop a year and a half ago was very nearly correct—'A little traitor, a little fool, and not much of anything.'"[39]

Pennypacker's admiration for Abraham Lincoln would survive for the remainder of his life. On the one hundredth anniversary of Lincoln's birth, February 12, 1909, he delivered an oration at the Historical Society of Pennsylvania, concluding, "The God who rules over the universe, holding the nations in the hollow of His hands and watching the fall of the sparrows, showed forth His loving kindness when to the American people he gave Abraham Lincoln."[40]]

---

as a major general in the Union army. In 1864, members of the Radical wing of the Republican Party tried to run him against Lincoln in the presidential election, but Frémont withdrew from the race in September 1864.

37. SWP to Aunt, Oct. 18, 1861, PM. SWP wrote a detailed account of his time in service in *Six Weeks in Uniform: Being the Record of a Term in the Military Service of the United States in the Gettysburg Campaign of 1863* (Schwenksville, PA: Pennypacker Mills, n.d.).

38. SWP to Grandfather, Sept. 19, 1863, PM.

39. SWP to Aunt, Oct. 18, 1863, PM.

40. *The Law Association of Philadelphia: Minutes of the Meetings and Exercises Held at the Rooms of the Historical Society of Pennsylvania, in Commemoration of the Centennial of the Birth of Abraham Lincoln. Orations by Hon. Samuel W. Pennypacker [and] Colonel Alexander K. McClure, February 12, 1909* (Philadelphia, 1909), 11.

Phoenixville
August 27th. 1864

Dear Sam,

As I am about to depart for College in a few days, & as I expect to be pretty busy immediately upon my arrival there, I take advantage of a portion of what remains of my loafing period, &—write you a letter. I have been desirous of doing so ever since your return to Philad. but, somehow, never managed to commence. I have just glanced over yours of the 24th. & find but one inquiry;—it is "Are you nearly bored to death?" Does it need an answer? You spent *one week* here, & I have spent eight, & if you were bored at the end of your *loaf,* what must be my present condition? Just think of it. Eight weeks; & in all that time, no variety excepting one or two boat rides. If these eight weeks were to be disposed of again I'll swear I would rather pass them laboring in the mill than *loafing.*

As to my studying the profession in the city. I think it quite probable that I will; but the assistance of which you speak would be all one sided. When I commence to study, you will be practicing. Father expects to bear the expense of my studies. *I* have determined that he *shall do nothing of the kind.* When I have graduated, I will consider that he has done enough in giving me an opportunity to obtain an education, or rather the foundation of one. I will be twenty one years of age a month or two before I become an *A.B.*[41] & from that time forth, will, to use a homely saying, "hoe my own row." So you see, some time must necessarily elapse before I can come to the city & commence my studies. In fact, if this war is once over, I may take a notion to go to Europe shortly after I graduate, & pass a few years there. If it were not for Annie, the possibility would be an absolute certainty.

The other day I bundled up all my letters, private documents, &c. "We do not know what a day may bring forth,"[42] & I would not like those things to be open to the inspection of any of the family: so I have left a note inside the bundle to the effect that the person opening the first wrapper should deliver the bundle, unopened, into your hands. If I chance to be drafted I will deliver it myself.[43] I hope you will have no objections to such an arrangement. The rebel bayonet & case which are now in the Reading Room, you may have, if you want them. I picked them up on the Antietam battle field.[44] I have also an order issued by a Virginia

41. SWP appears to have inserted a question mark in parentheses following "*A.B.*" Perhaps he did not realize that SMA was referring to a bachelor of arts degree.

42. Proverbs 27:1 states, "Boast not thyself of to morrow; for thou knowest not what a day may bring forth."

43. On March 3, 1863, Congress enacted the Enrollment Act, which made men between the ages of twenty and forty-five eligible for conscription into the army.

44. The Battle of Antietam, September 17, 1862, was the bloodiest day in American history.

Fig. 20. George W. Ashenfelter. (Courtesy of Pennypacker Mills, County of Montgomery, Schwenksville, PA)

general at the time of the John Brown excitement. George found it during his three months service in Virginia.—I think at Charlestown, Va.—& gave it to me shortly after his return. I will place them in Lloyd's hands, to be delivered to you, when you next come to Phoenix.[45]

I passed two hours with Annie on last Thursday evening, & for the first time in our lives we talked together of the future. The Church Choir had met for practicing, & Annie & I went down into the body of the church, & opening one of the windows, stood looking out over the quiet graves, talking & listening. We passed an evening there which I shall never forget. As we stood there, I

Although the battle essentially ended in a draw, Union forces stopped Lee's invasion into Maryland, forcing him to cross the Potomac River back into Virginia.

45. These items are no longer with SWP's papers at PM. Many of SWP's items were sold at auction by his children in 1920; other things wound up with the site's caretakers. SMA's older brother, George Washington Ashenfelter, served as a corporal in the 1st Pennsylvania Infantry, a three-month regiment that mustered into the service in 1861. Later he served as an officer in the 104th Pennsylvania Volunteers.

inwardly vowed that she should never have cause to regret the steps which, on my account, she had taken. If I ever break that vow, I will set myself down as unworthy [of] love friendship, or confidence, & act accordingly.

Your Friend

Sing Ashenfelter

Phoenixville

Aug. 29th, 1864

Dear Sam,

When I wrote the other day, I had intended to forward the enclosed.[46] As usual, it slipped my memory. As in every other group, I look just like a plug.

Your Friend

Sing Ashenfelter

[*Editors' Note:* On the night of Tuesday, August 30, Ashenfelter's friends "had a party out . . . to give Singleton a chance to accompany Annie once more before he left" for Dickinson.[47]]

Dickinson College

Sept. 26, 1864

Dear Sam,

The blue devils have been growing thicker & thicker for some days past until to-night, they are absolutely multitudinous. To raise my spirits I have tried every imaginable expedient, except the old one; & have tried them in vain. As a last resort, I sit down to write to you: not to reply to your last letter,—only to write to you because it will be a relief. I am just in that enviable state of mind which darkens every surrounding. For the three weeks just past, every evening has been spent with the ladies, &, as a natural result, I am tired of their society. Their conversations on the omnipresent subject of—somebody else, have become absolutely "borous." It may be very natural, but it is none the less disagreeable to find man's companion so closely wrapped up in trifles,—in petty jealousies[.]

Sept. 29.

Holmes says, "Do you want an image of the human will, or the self determining principle as compared with its prearranged & impassable restrictions?

46. The enclosure has not been located.

47. Horace Lloyd to SWP, Sept. 4, 1864, PM.

A drop of water imprisioned in a crystal; you may see such a one in any miner-alogical collection. One little fluid particle in the crystallein prison of the solid universe."[48] What do you think of it? You do not think he can be a believer in the Bible! Nor can any other *sensible* man. With me, it must come to something of that kind. Belief & non-belief cannot be reconciled; & either the vast body of other people entertain foolish views, or else *I* do. I cannot make such acknowl-edgement as to myself, & so it must fall upon others. Do not think me unjust; I believe all this & cannot persuade myself to the contrary. Christianity is such a monstrous absurdity that I am as intolerant as a puritan.

I quote, "All solids are made up of planes, planes of lines, & lines of points."[49] Cant admit anything of the kind. "A point is of necessity, nothing at all."[50] Just what I think—agree with you entirely. How many *nothings* must we combine in order to have *something*? A line is *not* made up of a certain number of points. You might add point upon point infinitely & you would still be very far from having a line; for, nothing added to nothing amounts to nothing. Nor is a plane made up of lines. You might place all the lines of which you can conceive side by side & still you would have nothing more than a line. It follows from the very nature of the thing—length without either breadth or thickness. Lines may represent the boundaries of planes, but they do nothing more. For these same reasons, solids are *not* made up of planes. I could never think of admitting that "matter is composed of a certain number of points":—atoms—if you will, but not *points*. I am of [the] opinion that matter is—everywhere; that even *mind* is matter. There's Materialism for you. How some good people would hold up their hands in holy horror if they knew the sentiments of those surrounding them. I know an Atheist at Dickinson who goes to the communion table every month; & I really cannot say that I think he does, thereby, a very great wrong.

Again I quote, "Excuse me for boring you with one of my difficulties[.]" Sam, Ink cost something these days, & paper is "viz," & so for the sake of economy, omit all such as the above from this time forth. Dont rob me of a line by insert-ing such a request as that. Seriously, that part of the letter was the most interest-ing, & when the "excuse me" met my eyes, it almost made me "cuss[.]"

As I had anticipated, I have been selected to deliver the anniversary address before our Society. A position of much honor—as students think: something borous & desirable—as I think. Borous because of the address, yet to be written—

48. This quotation comes from Oliver Wendell Holmes Sr., *The Autocrat of the Breakfast-Table: Every Man His Own Boswell* (1858; repr., Boston: Houghton, Mifflin, 1895), 86.

49. This quotation comes from Aristotle's *On the Heavens.* See W. K. C. Guthrie, ed., *On the Heavens* (Cambridge, MA: Harvard Univ. Press, 1960), 263.

50. This may be a quotation from SWP's earlier letter.

desirable, because students regard an anniversarian as an individual of considerable importance. It is the highest honor Society—Literary of course—can confer.

As to my resolution, it has grown stronger & stronger since the first time I refused to drink. How often I have refused, I cannot tell, but it is certain that *the boys* have ceased to invite. I cannot conceive of an inducement strong enough to set aside my determination. To tell the truth, I can hardly realize that I could ever have been such a fool. But an influx of visitors compels me to close.

Your Friend

Sing Ashenfelter.

Dickinson College

November 25. 1864

Dear Sam,

Almost two months since I last wrote to you. From Oct. 2. to Nov. 25., & really it seems to have been a year. *Why* I did not write I am at as much loss to tell as you, perhaps, to imagine. As excuses are below par with us, I will not attempt to conjure up a lie. Let *my* silence pass, as did *yours; in* silence. Before me are two letters, & a note of invitation. To the latter I had hoped to be able, ere this, to reciprocate, but as our committees on printing *will* be tardy, my hope was vain. The other two I will attempt to take in charge to-night; absenting myself from my lady friends for the first evening this session. Fortunately, the Senior Year turns out to be an exceedingly easy one. Not that we have fewer studies, but they are more equally distributed—allowing an hour for study before the most of them. And so we are relieved from the necessity of studying after night. I think I can say that, notwithstanding my intimacy with the ladies of Carlisle, I have made better recitations this session than ever before.

But, to your letters. What *were* the trying circumstances under which that of the 9th. inst. was written. I really could not understand. From the tenor of the letter itself I judged you to be somewhere in unpleasant proximity to a political speaker. From that of the 20th. I inferred that ladies were in the neighborhood. I do not wish to incense the sex, but I cannot refrain from indulging in the reflection that when anything is to be *done* both circumstances would be exceedingly trying. However, the letter was written, I received it, & notwithstanding your expectation to the contrary, found it both legible & interesting.

As to Stultorum,[51] I believe I discovered therein some twenty four errors. It

---

51. Albert H. Slape, *Stultorum: A Poem Delivered before the Belles Lettres and Union Philosophical Societies of Dickinson College, June 28, 1864* (Carlisle, PA, 1864). Slape was a member of the class of 1858.

Fig. 21. Albert H. Slape. (Courtesy of Archives and Special Collections, Dickinson College, Carlisle, PA)

was never designed for publication, & when read by the author was exceedingly amusing. By the way, can you tell me the political sentiments of the author. It was quite a question among those who only read the poem,—some judging this way—some that. He evidently avoids expressing them in Stultorum. Slape is the first lawyer of Salem, N.J. Not much in that, however.

Of all subjects under heaven, what do you suppose I have chosen for my anniversary address? Religious Liberty. Nor is this all: I am trying to oppose it. I was tempted so to do so [sic] through my dislike for popular opinions. As might have been expected I have signally failed to show any reason for such opinions as I attempt to maintain, or to advance any arguments which I myself could not refute with half the effort required in their construction. I am going to speak it though, for one half of the audience will not pay enough attention to know what I'm talking about; & the other half will regard it—& correctly—as words strung together to fill up the half hour—maximum,—fifteen minutes—minimum. I will send it to you *before* the anniversary—that is, if I am not to[o] lazy to make a copy of it—& expect you to read it, as written to be spoken, & *not* read.

I have not ceased to congratulate myself upon the result of the late political campaign. Everything, excepting right, was at stake, & common sense gained the day. I say everything but right because I do not think that element entered very deeply into either platform.[52] But you know my old opinions of government, & I will not trouble you by repeating them.

52. In the presidential election of 1864, the Democratic Party platform called the war a "failure" and focused on the Lincoln administration's restrictions of civil liberties. The Re-

For the last month I have been very patiently awaiting a letter from Lloyd. What has become of the youth. His silence is inexplicable. If you write to him soon, give him a quiet "rowing up" & tell him to charge it to my account. What I said as to that "proxy" business came from the idea or rather opinion that authority of that kind cannot properly be delegated. I am not particular, however, & if we can defeat Shaffer & his party by this means, all right. I told Lloyd I would not vote for the measure, but upon second thought, I have concluded to do so, if it is brought up while I am at home. I have not, as yet, definitely determined upon my course after graduation. I have an idea—a strange one you & most of others will think—which I can better communicate verbally. You will hear it next vacation, & in the mean time, you may, if you choose, exercise your imagination. My Chum is coming to Phoenix with me when I return, & you will then have an opportunity of knowing the youth, with whome I struck hands, on my advent at Dickinson. I expect to return about the 22nd, or 23rd. of December. If you see Ben. R.W. give him my regards.

Your Friend
Sing Ashenfelter.

publican platform called for reunion, the defeat of the Confederacy, and an amendment to the Constitution abolishing slavery. On November 8 Lincoln won reelection, defeating his Democratic opponent, Maj. Gen. George B. McClellan.

CHAPTER FOUR

1865

[*Editors' Note:* Horace Lloyd's relationship with Lide Vanderslice, which comes up throughout the 1865 correspondence, appears to have been the subject of a good deal of gossip among Ashenfelter and Pennypacker's circle of friends. Lloyd and Lide began to show interest in one another as early as October 1863, seeing each other as much as seven times per week.[1] But as will be seen below, Lide was quite unfaithful to him during their courtship. Lloyd must have sensed that some of his friends disapproved of their marriage, for he avoided them in the weeks leading up to the wedding, which took place on April 11, 1865. "Lloyd as you know has been married he acted very strange towards his friends," wrote Irvin J. Brower to Pennypacker. He complained that Lloyd "never said a word about it until the night before he was married then he said he would have told me but was so busy he did not get a chance until he thought I had heard of it." Brower, in fact, had known about the engagement for several weeks "but never said a word to him about his getting married either before or after and do not think I shall." Shortly after the wedding, Lloyd and Lide came to see Brower. He wrote of this visit: "Mrs Lloyd came up to me and gave me a good shake of the hand and I suppose she expected I would make a big time over her I never left [let?] on I knew they were married she then asked me to come over to see *us* it is *us* now and Lloyd said something about *us* two or three times."[2]

Pennypacker's mother could sense the tension regarding Lloyd's relationship with Lide. "You seem to think he might have done better," she wrote to her son, "perhaps you dont [like] her very well." But "if she is affectionate and amiable

---

1. Irvin Brower to SWP, Oct. [n.d.], 1863, PM.
2. Irvin Brower to SWP, Apr. 3, 23, 1865, PM.

and can make home pleasant for him, I suppose he dont care for any thing else." She continued, "Some men don't like very learned women, for my part I think, the husband ought always to be superior in knowledge—and the wife should be intelligent and have good common sense—and be acquainted with domestic duties."[3]

Some among the circle of friends opposed Lloyd's marriage because Lide was known for sleeping around. Pennypacker's brother Henry wrote, "He is a fool to marry her she is a horny king [kind?] of a girl I know by he[r] looks I guess she likes to be huged as well as any body."[4] In fact, Pennypacker's cousin Andrew R. Whitaker appears to have been sleeping with Lide during Lloyd's courtship of her. One of his letters to Pennypacker, from January 1864, is worth quoting at length:

It has been snowing this week, a great deal, and now there is very good sleighing but it don't do me any good as I have nary horse & sleigh, I would like to be at home now, and in a comfortable sleigh with Lloyds intended, and 2 or 3 others the names of whom it is needless to mention[.] I wonder if Mr Lord ever comes Home and then washes his fingers or hands after one of his customary visits? Between you and I, *she* told me he never did or thought of such a thing, I asked her if he played—that and a great many other things she told me one night, I had gone through the preliminary proceedings which are necessary to bring an amorous or any other girl, to a state, which by many is vulgarly called "hot," (you must excuse all of my dirty expressions,) and was progressing very nicely; when after a few remarks passing between us, she told me that which I have already told *you*, she in the mean time kept squirming, and pressing very tightly the hand which was unemployed, except now and then when it became necessary to further my advancement toward that goal of human happiness, from which we all return minus a "natty," either in its proper place in the moss covered cell or in our unmentionables. Fortunately I did not get worked up so much as all that, so I came out all OK, but for my partner in sin, I would not like to vouch, as I saw symptoms of—after an hour of this sort of bliss, she gave a mixture between a squirm and a stretch, then reposed very quietly in my arms and with flashing eyes, fairly liquid I might say, looked into mine. I guess about that time my "green orbs," sent forth a stream of fire, which answered hers, and answered any deficiency which might have occured before. To sum up I then gave and received a hot kiss, and came to the conclusion,—after it was all over—that I had been acting like a sick fool,

3. Anna Maria Whitaker Pennypacker to SWP, Apr. 14, 1865, PM.
4. Henry Clay Pennypacker to SWP, Apr. 2, 1865, PM.

anyhow that was about the last of the performance for that night, but I got such a very pressing invitation to come again, and to do likewise was understood of course—that I could not refuse, all the nonsense which she employed in asking me to come, would have been of no avail, if I had not known the tableau, in which I would have to act as one of the principal characters, I say that was the only inducement, and how Lloyd manages to spend 5 or 6 hours twice a week with her and not do any thing but talk and hug (he has got that far you know) I would like to know, I believe the boy will advance slowly but surely until he will make it a sure thing, then he will find to his sorrow that a s—f—k has no conscience.

Whitaker asked Pennypacker to "burn this letter after you have bored yourself reading it" and "commit it to the flames, with a prayer for the 'Hopeful,' who now subscribes himself."[5]

A few months later Whitaker again wrote to Pennypacker about Lide, calling her "that young lady who had more than one M—head, and perhaps she has a few more left, he [Lloyd] says *Miss Vanderslice.*" This reference to "more than one maidenhead" indicates that Lide was lying to Lloyd about being a virgin. Whitaker noted that she wanted his photograph and said that "if she gets one from me, it will not be my fault. There has been and very likely will be occasions when a person could not refuse *anything,* particularly when the '*corsets get broken*'"—another reference to his sleeping with Lide. Whitaker concluded his letter by telling Pennypacker that he had taken a pledge administered by a military officer "to not use tobacco in any form or drink any kind of liquor." He said that he "faithfully kept" the oath, "notwithstanding the many temptations from within and without," but was grateful that "the promise did not include cards and women." Whitaker then closed by telling his cousin that he was about to go to church—"there will be some 'lovelies' there who are very nice to look upon."[6]]

5. Andrew R. Whitaker to SWP, Jan. 9, 1864, PM. Whitaker sent SWP an even more ob-scene letter on November 27, 1864. It is unclear whether the girl he speaks of in this later letter was Lide, but it might have been since he describes her as having "nothing attractive about her except her personal charms."

6. Andrew R. Whitaker to SWP, Mar. 21, 1864, PM. Whitaker married Anna Maria Yerkes (1850–1924) in 1872; they had two children. Several postwar letters indicate that Yerkes had shown romantic interest in both SMA and SWP in the mid-1860s and that SMA was tempted to reciprocate her advances. See SMA to SWP, Oct. 26, 1868, Jan. 29, 1869, PM.

Phoenixville
Jan. 5. 1865

Dear Sam,

So much of a letter is always written without any difficulty, but what, in this, is to follow, I know not. As I am in Phoenix, however, it is possible to allude to topics in which our interest is mutual. In the first place, I am brought to a stand by Lloyd & his—well, I can call it nothing but d—d folly. From all that I can hear, Lide is preparing for marriage, & I believe firmly that they are engaged. As I intend to tell the youth, he is a cussed fool if he expects me to believe his story, when he knows it to be controverted by the sober facts of the case. I take it that Lloyd is a man of some honor, & I know that, unless he has some serious intentions his ideas & mine, upon that subject, are not coincident. Despite *his* assurances to the contrary, I feel confidant that Lide firmly expects to be Mrs. Lloyd, & the youths conduct, I think, has been such as to warrant such expectation.

As you will doubtless remember, I said to you last week that I did not think Lloyd would make money an object. I am almost prepared to reverse that opinion, for, in thinking the matter over, I can find *no other* object. I do not see how he can love her, & as far as *sensual* enjoyment is concerned, a man of sense would look elsewhere. I do not think matters would ever have gone so far, had we all remained in Phoenix., but Lloyd could not endure the opposition, & was compelled to seek other society; even at the risk—to use a vulgar expression— of jumping "from the frying pan into the fire." Perhaps it is not exactly right, though, to thus enter into a discussion of a friend's motives. Even though I say nothing which I would not repeat before him, yet I may be wrong & he right. I leave the riddle to the solution of time, acknowledging myself puzzled. I reserve, however, the right to give Lloyd an occasional assurance that he is a darned fool. If he marries her, I'll make it d—d fool.

I called on Annie last Tuesday evening and we had a very pleasant chat. She rather surprised me by asking whether the letters which I wrote to Father— somewhat carefully written, you know—were not designed to answer two purposes. Father & Dave Euen are quite intimate, & I had requested the former not to show my letters; in the full consciousness that the request would not be complied with. How Annie suspected the truth, I cannot imagine; I had not given her credit for looking so far. I have no doubt David has his suspicions too, but it is devilish little I care. When I come home after graduation I will be twenty-one years of age & shall take the first possible opportunity to speak with him upon the subject nearest my heart. My course of action towards the young lady in question must be then & there decided. Not that I will submit if he opposes us, but,—affairs must assume some definite position. I wait until I am twenty-one

Fig. 22. Class of 1865 outside of West College, ca. 1865. Ashenfelter sits at the front on the far left. (Courtesy of Archives and Special Collections, Dickinson College, Carlisle, PA)

because I do not care to act while there is an authority over my actions higher than my own. However, I commenced this letter with the intention of devoting it to affairs in which interest was mutual, I do not suppose the last page could be included under such a head. You have been, perhaps, already too much bored with such topics.

I am just thinking of writing a speech opposed to Universal Suffrage. Opposing it upon the ground that the object of government should be the greatest good to the greatest number; & that the legislation of the ignorant is not apt to produce that result—that the educated can rule the ignorant with happier results, than they—the ignorant—can rule themselves. There is humbug in the whole business, but it may do for a college speech. We get five nine-marks for a speech—that is, of course, if it merits a perfect mark.

Do not suppose that I have forgotten that I owe you a lengthy letter. The debt shall be cancelled, when plenty of time & inclination are coincident.

Until which time I am, on *one* sheet, none the less

Your Friend

Sing Ashenfelter

Phoenixville

Jan. 10, 1865

Dear Sam,

"The last shall be first";[7] the last *was* first, & *"between two sheets"* as it met my eye, upon drawing your last sheet from the envelope, was provokingly comical— so much so, much so—d—n it—that I startled a peaceable company by a most unequivocal & sonorous *smile.* I have no doubt I was regarded as rude in the extreme. Your fault you know. We *do* both agree that Lloyd is a fool, & I am try- ing every day to bring him to the same opinion. But, at every assurance of the fact, he will take to stroking his beard, &, in a provokingly matter-of-fact tone ejaculate, "Hem! Do you think so?" He did say, once, "well, maybe I *am* making a darned fool of myself." But what does that amount to? Last night, when Lide was asked to go skating by moonlight, she "did not know until she had seen *Horry*"; &, when once on the ice she "wondered if that old meeting at the Read- ing Room would not break up, pretty soon, so that *Horry* could come"; & at last, "there's Horry," & they were inseperable for the rest of the evening. I skated off, thinking involuntarily, "not all the d—d fools are dead, yet."

Perhaps, as the preachers say, it is a bad thing to have too little conscience; but, Great Heavens, that is nothing to possessing *too much* of an article of so questionable a value. I have some times thought that I am an excellent example of those whome the preachers afor[e]said would hold up, to show *how* bad a thing this lack is. However that may be, the *too much* will undoubtedly apply to Annie. The young lady has been worrying because, she told her father, some three years since, that she had *not* promised to write to me, & further because she did write to me while in New York. She seriously intended to explain the whole matter to David—which, by the way, I would have been very willing for at any other time than the present—& only awaited my return in order that she might first speak to me. Had it been a few months, either in the past or future, I would have been pleased to have let Euen know, in this way, what his opposition amounts to; but just at present it does not suit, & so I tried to dis- suade Annie from doing anything like that which she had intended. It took a whole afternoon to convince her of what I honestly believe—that duty did not require her to make such explanations. She surprises me every day by display- ing a knowledge of my doings, not only in Phoenixville, but in Carlisle; indeed she knows too much for me to believe it to be all surmise. That some one who knows me & dislikes me informs her, directly or indirectly, of my actions, I am

7. An allusion to Matthew 20:16: "So the last shall be first, and the first last: for many be called, but few chosen."

absolutely convinced. I believe that this individual has some sort of communication with Carlisle, for she has told me of things which I am confidant I never
spoke of in Phoenixville. The whole thing is an inigma to me; & I would give a
year of my existence to know who it is that has so deep an interest in my affairs.
I'll find out, some time.

Dont you think that in sinking your plummet for Andy's motive in voting
for Father O'Farrel[8] you went too deep? You were seeking for something tan-
gible where it did not exist. The whole thing, I think, was the result of an idea.

Andy is sufficiently skeptical to regard one church as just about as good as
another; & being almost without predjudice a natural feeling of opposition
would induce him to support one against whome so many were predjudiced.
He I think, felt that many opposed O'Farrel for the very poor reason that he was
a catholic, & his vote was a convincing proof to himself, if not to others, that he
was above such predjudice. I reason from analogy, for I came very near voting
for O'Farrel myself.

I did not mean that you should take [the] remark of mine,—as to being too
confidential,—to yourself. If I had thought of *applying* it to you, do you suppose
I would have *said* it to you. I think I would have to be exceedingly confidential
in doing that. As you know I say to you more than prudence would allow me to
say to anyone else; so dont talk to me about "concealing everything that I think
necessary[.]"

Now, I am going to tell you something of yourself that I do not believe you
suspect. In conversation, especially with ladies, your expression of countenance
is such as would lead one to suppose that you were weighing critically & holding up to internal ridicule everything said. So much so that I once heard a lady
ask "Dont Sam Pennypacker make fun of everything a body says?" Tell me, did
you ever suspect that such an expression lurks about your eyes?

Finally, curse this paper, this cloudy day for insufficient light, this pen, this
ink, this—everything. I have succeeded in dispatching a scrawl almost unintel-
ligable to myself. I go to Carlisle next Tuesday.

Write soon to
Your Friend
Sing Ashenfelter

---

8. Philip A. O'Farrell (1813–69) was born in Dublin, Ireland, and ordained a Roman Catholic priest in Philadelphia in 1844. He served as rector of St. Mary's Church in Phoenixville
from 1847 until his death. It is unclear what election SMA is referring to here.

Dickinson College

Jan. 23. 1865

Dear Sam,

Once more I hail you from Dickinson; &, in doing so, I almost feel as though it were for the last time. I never felt that the time for my final departure from College was drawing near until this last return to Carlisle; but now I look forward to my stay as brief indeed. I hardly knew that I had formed any strong attachments in my stay here until the close of last session, when I experienced a feeling of regret at the necessities which compelled departure. I hate anything which breaks in upon an accustomed routine, & verily, felt a strong inclination to forego seeing my friends & to remain in Carlisle during vacation. You know, Phoenix. is terribly dry, & *I* know Carlisle is just the opposite, so while the vacation promised a pleasant beginning, the close looked anything but tempting. My expectations were *not* disappointed, & had it not been for Annie, I know not what I would have done to pass the time. At any rate, as I said above, here I am again, &, being here, I write to you.

We are having the cursedest *white* weather that I ever experienced. Two snow storms since my return, & the third in course of operation. Flakes are descending in such innumerable quantities as to render objects at thirty yards distance almost invisable. To tell the truth, I feel more like cursing than writing; & were you now present I could communicate my thoughts much more *emphatically*, if not more fully to the satisfaction of all concerned.

That communication relative to *internal criticism* &c. must have produced quite a startling effect. I had not supposed that you would care much what your countenance indicated, so long as you preserved "mens sibi conscia recti,"[9] & alluded to the matter as something which I had frequently noticed, but never regarded as of paramount importance. If your *phiz*[10] tells a lie, I would suggest, as the best remedy, that a proper notice of the fact be placarded upon a conspicuous part of the offending member; but I pray you, do not regard the matter as being productive of any very considerable evil.

Annie & I spent some pleasant hours together during the days immediately preceding my departure. I spent Monday evening alone with her, & of course we talked much upon our own affairs. If you had heard us you would have considered the *five dollars* dependent upon a certain event, as already yours. But the matter is yet in doubt, & I seriously advise you not to make any provision

---

9. Latin for "a mind aware of its own rectitude" or "a mind aware of what is right." This quotation originally comes from Virgil's *Aeneid*.

10. An informal word for a person's face or expression.

for the investment of the amount until the final step is taken. I *may* win, even yet. You know *David* does not bid fair to be of any assistance to your side of the question, & unless you "buy him over" *my* chances are not so bad.

I had a long talk with Lloyd before I left, as regards his affairs with Lide. He did not seem to think that she regarded him in any other light than that of a friend. I think I convinced him to the contrary, &, if I am not mistaken, the aspect of affairs will change somewhat. I would not like to see him marry her, & although I do not believe her capable of any very deep feelings, I told him that in my opinion, he was doing wrong. If he does not marry her, most of the people in Phoenixville, & more especially her relatives, will blame him for triffling with the young lady; & I assured him that, although he might feel so very independent, he would find that state of affairs anything but agreeable. Mail closes, write soon.

Your Friend
Sing Ashenfelter

Dickinson College
Jan. 25, 1865

Dear Sam,

I write to trouble you with a commission. The occupants of No. 50 are in want of seals, & I am placed under the necessity of asking you to procure them for us, as you are the only person in Philadelphia who is well known to either of us. The style desired is about as follows. Cylindrical brass dies, about one inch in length, & with a diameter of an ordinary wafer. They may be either with or without handles. Three is the number desired, bearing the initials H. M. & A. respectively:—which are supposed to represent Himes, Mills,[11] Ashenfelter. The one bearing my initial I wish cut in Old English text. My roommates have just come in & say they want theirs done up in the same style.

I am sorry to trouble you in this, but if you will procure them & send me the bill, you will confer a favor on

Your Friend,
Sing Ashenfelter.

11. Fairfax Oaks Mills (1845–66) of Altoona, Pennsylvania, was a sophomore at Dickinson and lived in West College, Room 50, with SMA and Himes. Mills was a member of the Phi Kappa Sigma fraternity with SMA but died before he could graduate from the college.

Dickinson College

Jan. Dont Know. 1865

Dear Sam,

Your letter came to hand yesterday, & made me smile audibly. I think we are becoming remarkably obtuse: for certain it is that my latest remarks relative to *internal criticism* were intended to be taken as *ironical. Of course* it is all "gammon," (Irony, D—n it) but then, still, we have expended considerable ink & paper upon it. One would'n't suppose that you gave so trivial a matter a second thought.—Devilish Ironical—

But, as to the seals. Here is the best way that I can indicate what is wanted. First, by answering your inquiry by saying that the "inch long cylinder" is just what I meant; & secondly, by giving the following *exceedingly artistic* sketch— irony, as to the words underscored—

The Dies may be of any length, so that they will set in the handles, be it an inch or a nail.[12] The handles any shape you choose, so that they may be taken hold of. Suit your own taste & I will answer for ours. I will reply to your letter when I have more time. For the present, farewell.

Your Friend

Sing Ashenfelter

P.S. If you can find a translation to the Clouds of Aristophanes,[13] Please send it to me when you send the seals; I enclose the cost of the whole.

Your Friend

Idem*

Dickinson

Same Date

Dear Sam,

I sent a note to you this morn &, as might be expected, forgot something. When you send the seals, please send three sticks of good sealing wax. We cannot procure a good article in Carlisle.

Your Friend

Sing Ashenfelter

12. The word "nail" once also referred to a measure of length for cloth equal to two and a quarter inches.

13. Authored by famous Athenian comic playwright Aristophanes (446–386 BC), *The Clouds* mocked Socrates as an eccentric and pretentious teacher.

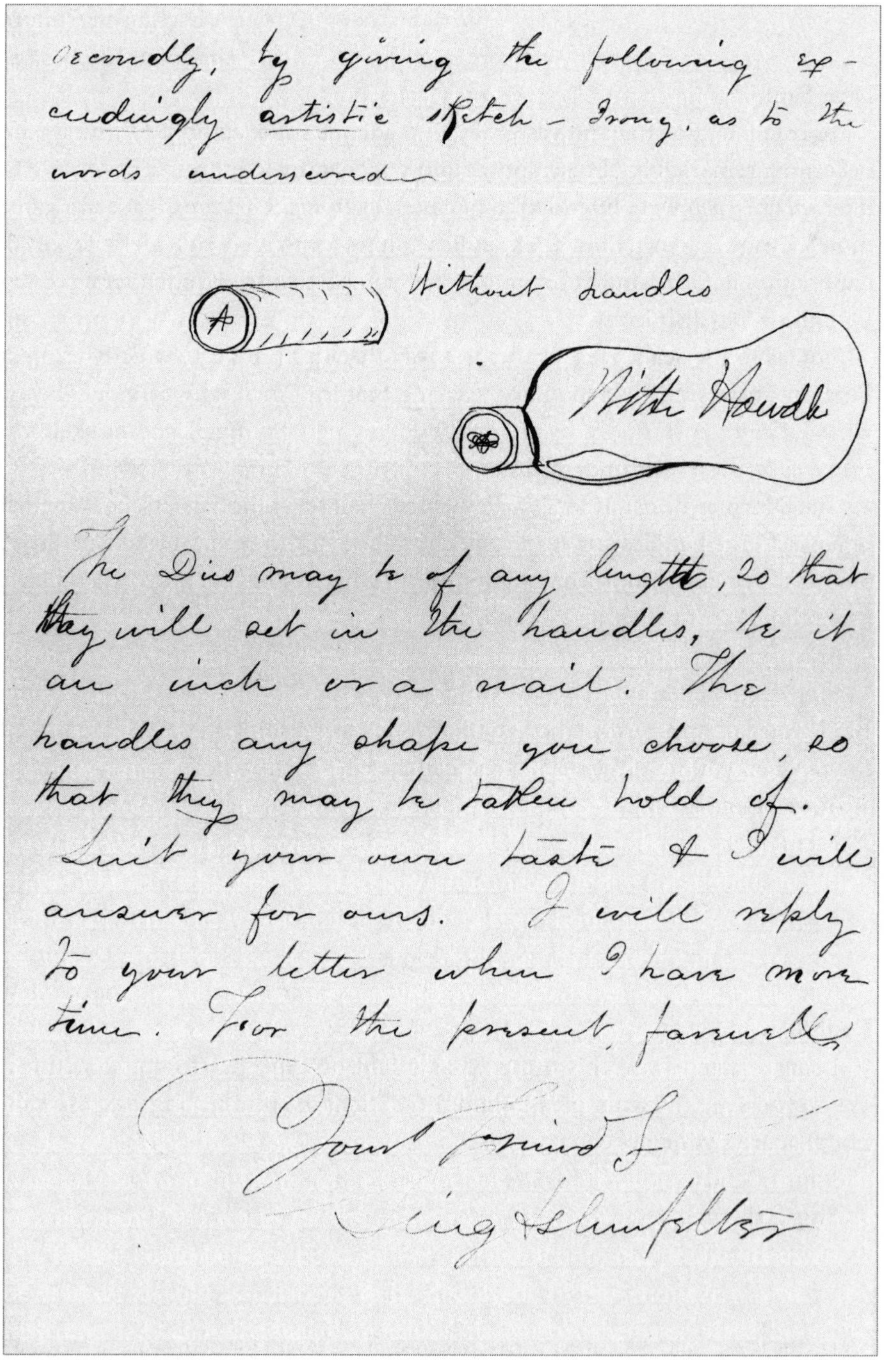

Secondly, by giving the following exceedingly artis*tic sketch – I*rony. *as to the words underscored—*

Without handles

With Handle

The Dies may be of any length, so that they will set in the handles, be it an inch or a nail. The handles any shape you choose, so that they may be taken hold of. Suit your own taste & I will answer for ours. I will reply to your letter when I have more time. For the present, farewell

Your friend

Aug Ashenfelter

Fig. 23. Ashenfelter drew this picture of the dies he requested in his letter to Pennypacker dated "Jan. Dont Know. 1865." (Courtesy of Pennypacker Mills, County of Montgomery, Schwenksville, PA)

Dickinson College

Feb. 2, 1865

Dear Sam,

Please send me Ben Whitaker's directions at your earliest possible convenience & oblige,

Your Friend

Sing Ashenfelter

P.S. You will have quite a stock of notes on hand soon if ideas continue to strike your most obedient in this disconnected manner

Idem

[*Editors' Note:* The following letter is largely nonsensical, as Ashenfelter acknowledges at the end.]

Dickinson College

Feb. 10. 1865.

Dear Sam,

First, what the devil to say. Secondly, how the devil to say it. Not that the former occasions any *real* difficulty beyond the decision of preference but that there is a liability of falling upon what *might* be construed in a sense opposed to the intention. Then as to preference. If the tenor of my remarks is liable to be misunderstood, then I am especially anxious to touch upon nothing of an important nature. If, for instance, I were to remark that *Phoenixville is an elegant*[14] *place in which to pass a few leisure months,* I could not rest satisfied until I had definitely ascertained that you had not deserted your legal studies for a lengthy sojourn in that pleasant rural district. Then, I dare not touch upon the weather, for fear that you will be equally absurd with myself & waste a half sheet of good letter paper in commenting upon that "remarkable phenomenon[.]" Internal criticism wont do, because it is regarded by the individual who should be most deeply interested, "as—well—gammon." In short, I am completely nonplussed & cannot decide what to say *first,* as being least likely to be misunderstood. You can see, then, the importance of my *secondary;* or, how the devil to say it.

Now the question arises, is an ironical remark reprehensible, as being, in reality false? The decision of this point requires that we go back to the original genus action, of which this is a species. Now every action is divided into four distinct elements: or, rather "four distinct elements may be observed in every action. They are 1st. The conception of the act. 2nd. The resolution to carry that conception

14. This word is underlined three times.

into effect. 3rd. The out-ward act. 4th. The *intention* or *design* with which all this is done[.]"[15] Let us suppose the existence of three individuals, named for convenience A, B, & C. Now, let us suppose—understand me, it's *only* a supposition—A & B to give C an amount of money. They both had a clear conception of this act. They both mentally resolved to carry their conceptions into effect; & they both did so. As yet, we can see nothing wrong in either. But suppose A to have given the money for the purpose of relieving the poor, & B for the purpose of bribing C to commit murder: then, the evil becomes evident—we see it in the *intention*.

Now, as there is no *intention to deceive* in an ironical remark, the same is not reprehensible, as embodying a falsehood, in its criminal sense. What remains then is to express irony in such a manner, as to place its identity beyond question. In doing or rather, attempting to do this *I* seem to have failed most signally. This failure recoiled upon me with a most stunning* effect; it made me the recipient of a letter in the construction of which a quill was driven "with the express purpose of pitching into the last two letters received, &c[.]" Is it any wonder that, having once decided that I have something to say, & further, having definitely determined what that something might be; is it any wonder I say, that I should hesitate, as to the manner in which it should be said. If irony should be mistaken for earnestness, or earnestness for irony, how futile would be all my efforts to make myself understood. And how unsatisfactory to the recipient, a letter so awkwardly constructed as to leave him in doubt as to the authors meaning. All these things make me hesitate. I am especially anxious that every thing I say or write may have the effect which *I* intend & not be liable to optional construction. This is the case generally; but here, in this epistle, I desire more than ever before, to be clear, plain, & easily understood. Now the hesitation which I expressed upon the other page, must of necessity be increased when I consider these things last mentioned: for I know that anyone who is naturally liable to obscurity of style must inevitably develope this awkward tendency when he makes special exertions to avoid every thing of the kind.

Now, having given you a brief statement of my mental condition, I will occupy the *body* of this letter in referring to the subjects which have placed my mind in such a state of perturbation. Many thanks. You need take no farther trouble as to Aristophanes. A copy has been procured from Harvard & I can manage to get along by using it between hours, although it does not belong to me. I close with a quotation from your letter. "When you are hard pushed, why dont you adopt my style & talk nonsense." Your Friend,

Sing Ashenfelter

15. This quotation comes from Francis Wayland, *The Elements of Moral Science,* rev. ed. with notes by Joseph Angus (1835; London: Religious Tract Society, 1858), 10.

Dickinson College
Feb. 11. 1865

Dear Sam,

Your letter, express receipt, bill, seals &c. all came to hand this morning[.]
We are perfectly suited & return many thanks. The amount of expenditure in
this affair is I believe as follows.

Seals	$3.75
Wax	.60
Express	.50
Two Letters	.06
	$4.93[16]

Dont care to forward half a pound of postal currency.[17] Enclosed is amount.

Your Friend

Sing Ashenfelter

[On back of page:] I wrote to you a day or two ago.

Dickinson College
Feb. 1865

Dear Sam,

I sit down this afternoon to do that in regard to which my intention has so
long been good—i.e., reply to your letter of the 16th. of May, 1864. This matter
should have been attended to at a much earlier date, but—you know my old
habits of procrastination:—every thing deferred until the last moment, & then,
usually, about half accomplished. Perhaps, however, the year which has elapsed,
may have developed new opinions, or, at least, new modes of viewing old subjects, so that, with a better light, we may be able to judge of all things with more
justice & accuracy.

You will doubtless remember that one of the prominent matters under discussion at that writing was your correspondence with Miss Alice Lee. You never gave
me any direct denial of my assertions, or rather, insinuations, relative to the matter, but turned the question by disserting upon the unreliability of "village gossip,"—upon which our opinions are coincident—& stigmatizing the whole matter
as "bosh," "gammon" &c. The nearest approach to anything definite occurs in the
closing sentences of your letter. I give them just as written. "On reperusing this

16. Note that the total should have been $4.91.

17. Postal currency, which were paper notes featuring images of stamps, were issued in
1862 and 1863 after Northerners began hoarding metal coinage. The image of a stamp provided confidence that the paper currency had actual value.

letter I still have some fear that you will misconstrue that Alice Lee matter, & not wishing to be misunderstood, I give you my word that, if ever I get into a scrape of that kind, I will let you know about it forth with." Very good, is my comment, but while very explicit as to the future, it would hardly include the case of the then past & present. Such a correspondence may never have existed, or may have been of a purely *friendly* nature; Andy's & my laughs upon the letter of *seven pages* may have had no foundation more secure than our own conjectures; I may have been mistaken in the meaning of the individual from whom my information was drawn, or that individual may not have had the best of authority for the thing said. I say all these things *may have been,* but—it's hardly likely. I dont wish you to imagine that I say these things, soliciting confidence; I trust that you would not give me credit for so low a motive; I say them merely as a means of accounting for what might otherwise seem to be a stubbornness of opinion. You remember we had a discussion as to whether that subject did really occupy a page of your letter. Although the decision then was in my favor, the things said & to be said do not seem to have been entirely exhausted; for I find, upon reference, that even more space has been taken up *here* than I had thought of placing to your credit *there.*

The good people of Carlisle say that I am engaged to be married, & you must not be surprised when I tell you that, for once, *"village gossip"* is *apparently* well founded. I am about to tell you what no one else than myself knows; so brace your patience to hear how a *Friend* has violated what the world & perhaps you would call his honor. If there has been developed in me within the past year one inclination or rather, one passion, higher than any other, it is that for the study of character. I have neglected College duties, I have made myself a hypocrite, I have—I was almost about to say, violated confidence of friends, all for the sake of gratifying my wish to see human character in all its possible aspects. But perhaps I can be more intelligable if I "tell you all about it[.]"

Almost my first lady acquaintance in Carlisle was a Miss Alice Rheem.[18] I met her in the latter part of my Sophomore Year, & we very soon became good friends. Nothing disturbed the even tenor of our ways until about a year afterwards when, having concluded that her actions meant something more than friendship, I proposed:—to satisfy my curiosity, partially, but I must acknowledge, somewhat influenced by other feelings. My curiosity was satisfied for Alice acknowledged her feelings. When I had left her, & my reason became paramount I saw the folly of what I had done, & would have immediately endeavored to right the wrong & make all reparation in my power, had I not been restrained by a stronger & I must acknowledge, a less laudable inclination. *I wanted to study her character.*

18. Alice Rheem's father, Jacob, was a member of the college's board of trustees.

Aided by a relationship so intimate as was ours, I had, of course a most excellent opportunity for doing this. I soon discovered that her supreme trait was
selfishness. You may be surprised that I had not discovered this at an earlier moment, but she had so many visitors, more especially from among the students,
that I had but seldom met her alone, & then only for a short time. Indeed in
making my declaration to her I had trusted almost as much to what I had heard
of her saying as to my own observation. A young lady friend of hers, who is of a
very confidential sort of creature aided me very materially. As I said I found her
to be supremely selfish—so much so, that it relieved my uncomfortable position of much embarrassment. I discovered that she was ambitious, that she had
dabbled in metaphysics & was decidedly skeptical, that, in fact, she was just such
a woman as would sacrifice all tender feeling whenever & wherever it stood between what [sic] her & what she considered her advantage. It took me sometime
to discover what her friends had not suspected, & then, how to get myself out
of the scrape with apparent honor. It is possible that she may have been fooling
with me, just as I was with her. In fact I am almost inclined to think that such
was the case; for I did not find that my efforts at separation met with any very
determined resistance. I told her first, just what my prospects were. She replied
that she could wait until I had reached a secure position. I told her to think well
before she staked her future upon a chance which I myself regarded as doubtful.
She again replied, "I know of no student whose chances are better than your's;
the Junior Contest is regarded as a fair test of ability & every one says that you
will take the Gold Medal.["]

That conversation was just a day or two before the Contest. My speech was
written & in the hands of the Committee on Examination. Too late for any thing
in that direction. I did not dare to attempt to take a prize, & so I must depreciate
my standing by poor declamation. The first remark that saluted me on leaving
the stage was made by Prof. Wilson. "Why, Ashenfelter you hav'nt done yourself
justice." To which I replied "I know it, but I've done what I wished to do." A very
thoughtless remark on my part. Well, to sum up all, in composition, the maximum mark was one hundred; my mark was ninety-eight—I stood first. In declamation, the maximum being the same, my mark was forty-nine, being the lowest
on the scheme. So the gold & silver medals went elsewhere, & your most humble
had the honor of occupying the third position, in the general summing up.[19]

19. SMA delivered this speech on June 27, 1864. It is reproduced in Appendix D. Professor
Wilson died shortly after SMA wrote this letter. On February 22 he prepared a new will, then
died early on the morning of March 2, leaving behind a son and a daughter. Augusta Lutie
Johnson (1844–1900), daughter of the college's president, stated: "It was but little more than

Commencement week passed by, & the morning previous to that of our departure the result was made known in the Chapel, & I do not believe anyone congratulated the successful contestants with more hearty good will than did your most humble, aforesaid. I spent that evening at a ball at Papertown, a few miles from Carlisle, but neither Alice nor myself made any allusion to the Contest. I was silent because I wanted absence to work its influence before I broached the subject again; & I presume pride kept her from saying anything. When I bade her farewell, next morning, I fancied I could perceive beneath her apparent affection, a something which she sought to hide. Did it never occur to you during last summer vacation that I had something on my mind, beyond Annies mere discovery of my bad habits. I was tempted then to tell you all this but did not dare to, for fear that I might never be able to release myself. If I had not, you would never have known what you now know. But, to close this somewhat tedious narration, when I came back to Dickinson to commence my Senior Year I went into Rheem's house with many misgivings. Miss Alice was dressing, & her older sister was in the parlor. The young lady herself soon made her entrance. Fortunately Mary's presence prevented all demonstration at first meeting.[20] She soon left however, & then a conversation of about an hours length ensued. We went over the whole matter & when I left the house, it was with a light heart, *for we had concluded to be nothing more than very good friends.*

So much for that trouble. I was well out of it, & if nothing else had been effected, I had at least learned a lesson. If I am ever so thoughtless again, I will conclude that I am indeed a fool. But, as to the rumor of my engagement. About the beginning of last Session I met a young lady named Sue Cathcart.[21] She was introduced to me, or rather, I to her, by her most intimate lady friend. We became well acquainted in a short time, & I soon fell into the habit of spending

---

two weeks, before his death, that he acknowledged himself sick enough to take his room, and then he almost immediately commenced the final arrangements of his business. Though painful to his friends to feel that it must be done, it was well he undertook it so early for the last days of his life he suffered much." Following Wilson's death, the entire campus and local community grieved. "How sorrowfully the tolling of the College bells fell upon the ears and hearts of all Carlisle, and Emory Church was filled with those who came to pay the tribute of respect to one who was so well known and then we followed his remains to the graveyard; there all covered with snow." Lutie to Asbury J. Clarke, Mar. 13, 1865, collection of Jonathan W. White. The Faculty Minutes paid tribute to Wilson: "As a Professor and College Officer, his fidelity and earnestness are worthy of the highest praise. As a friend & associate, his unaffected sincerity & his excellent Christian Character endeared him to his Colleagues, and made him a welcome guest in their families."

20. Mary C. Rheem (1838–78) was Alice's older sister.

21. Susan L. Cathcart (1840–89) of Carlisle was the daughter of a widower and wealthy merchant. She appears to have died unmarried.

almost every evening in her company. When I next see you I will show you the photographs of five young ladies. They comprise the set of girls with whome Miss Sue is intimate; & I class them all as my best friends in Carlisle. Three of them I particularly admire; prominent among whome is the young lady in question.

I like her for her kind heart & her almost entire freedom from deceit. I have been intimate with her for more than six months & have yet to hear her make any unfavorable personal comment, even where persons persue a course of conduct entirely opposed to what she regards as right. If she sees a student drunk she pities him but never makes a public remark upon the circumstance. I never detected in her the least attempt at deceit, either direct or indirect. She has faults, of course, prominent among which is an inordinate sensitiveness & a liability to misconstrue many things said innocently into personalities. People say we are engaged because I am almost always in her company: in reality, there is no foundation for the rumor. I think Miss Sue & I understand each other entirely. Nothing of a tender nature has ever passed between us, & nothing ever shall. We are very intimate friends but nothing else. If the young lady feels otherwise, then she has more talent for concealing her true feelings than the most of the sex. My opportunities for observation have been most excellent, & I feel assured that I do her no wrong in maintaining our present relationship. Her confidant, I feel assured, knows exactly how matters stand, but the rest of the set think as does the public: i.e.—that we are engaged. I do all this, firstly, because I am very fond of the society of these young ladies, & secondly, because it affords many opportunities of reading character, when subject to very little or no restraint: for they regard me almost as one of their own sex.

Now, having told you all this, I wish to assure you that my feelings towards Annie are as strong as ever, & if I ever lose my bet of five dollars, she *alone* will be to blame. You said in one of your late letters that you had often felt tempted to reveal to me something more than you were accustomed of your inner nature. Did it not seem to you during the winter vacation, that I was several times on the point of saying what second thought restrained? One day in particular, we were both on the sofa, & the temptation to tell you all this was so strong that I was prevented from so doing only by the fear that it would not meet with sympathy or interest. I live in the hope that this lengthy narration will not bore you.

Time has developed at least the partial truth of your old theory as to Lloyd's conduct & motives. He would be both glad & sorry to be relieved of his present incubus—Lide.[22] Glad, because he would feel easier in mind, &—as I know from

---

22. SMA likely meant succubus, a female demon that has sexual intercourse with a sleeping man, as opposed to incubus, a male demon that does so to a woman, unless he was making a snide remark about Lide's physical appearance.

experience—could face every man without feeling assured that he was thought to be "dead in love." Sorry, because it would break in upon established habits, & would nullify the fire & keep him in the frying pan,—i.e. Y.M.L.U. He talks quite awkwardly when that subject is introduced &, on the whole, seems to feel quite uncomfortable. I am confident that he is now convinced that Lide looks upon him as something more than a friend. If I can take his word for it, he has never entertained the most remote idea of marrying her. Now, here I go, thoughtlessly pitching into Lloyd's course of conduct when my own is almost identical with it;—even worse, for, to all outward appearances, I have *two* strings to my bow. I wonder what Lloyd would think if he were to hear some of the Carlisle gossip. However there is decidedly more attraction about Miss Sue than there is about Lide, & so you would not have to wonder what motive I *could* have. But, as I have said, *we* understand each other; Lloyd & Lide I am sure, do not. Before we leave Lloyd I wish to ask whether there is not a slight feeling of coolness between you two, & whether your correspondence has not ceased?

I now reaffirm what you did not think I meant in a former letter; viz. what the world calls principle, I hold in utter contempt. I mean it just as I write it. My standerd of right & wrong differs from yours in that it is concerned with pleasure rather than law. You say that acting in accordance with certain immutable laws is right—in opposition, is wrong. I think whatever contributes to my pleasure is right:—all else,—wrong. That is, the standard is individual in its nature. I dont think I should ask whether a certain act would be beneficial to the race; if I can be satisfied that it would be of advantage to self, that is sufficient for me. In just so far as aiding the race satisfies my predjudices, or in any way gives me pleasure, I am willing to lend a helping hand; but not one step farther. This may seem a very narrow minded policy, but it is only a plain statement of what is universal. I think that in everything man estimates the accruing pleasure from participation. With me the case is especially strong. I recognize no Supreme Power & consequently feel that I owe no higher duty than to self. For instance, I am ready to contend that I did no wrong in all my transactions with Miss Alice Rheem: because the whole matter resulted to my advantage then & taught me a lesson which may be of advantage hereafter. In short what the world calls policy is my principle:—which this communication violates.

Now, dont imagine that these views will make me a rascal. I think that, just in proportion as evil advances, must all honest men suffer. The predominance of rascality would very materially affect my happiness, & consequently, is something in no way desirable. From this you can see that not only is what the world calls policy my principle, but also, what the world calls principle becomes, on account of its results, my policy. Which may be supposed to mean, that if I live according [to] principle I do so merely because such a course of action will conduce to my happiness. I do not wish you to imagine that I am attempting to present this matter in the form of an argument. I only intend it as a simple statement of my somewhat peculiar & of course unpopular views.

Speaking of unpopular views reminds me of the fact that I have come to the conclusion that Universal Suffrage is both wrong & inexpedient[.] You know, there is a certain class of subjects which the masses watch with extreme jealousy. They are regarded as having the most important bearing upon public welfare because their influence is both direct & immediate. They are such as express ideas which popular predjudice has made apparently essential to good government. Now, predjudice is an evil; & when an evil of this nature becomes popular it is all the more difficult to eradicate from the fact that each individual finds *his* opinions supported by those of his neighbor. Hence, in the consideration of such subjects as that of Universal Suffrage we should not allow these facts to escape our observation—that that [sic] the popular predjudice & more especially the predjudice of the ignorant is in its support, & that all investigations must be conducted in the face of the bitterest opposition.

But a question upon which opinions have been & still are so varied as this must certainly have some weight of argument upon both sides. Differences so great cannot be causeless; & although the masses would cry down anything like an attack upon their predjudices, yet it behooves none the less to ascertain, if possible, whether the tendencies of such ideas as that of Universal Suffrage are towards good or evil. You know, a government is good or evil just in proportion as its rulers are intelligent & virtuous or ignorant & vicious. We lay it down as a general truth that civilization & good government advance hand in hand, & whatever tends to retard the one has an equal influence upon all. The greater the power of ignorance & vice, the lower must be the tone of the organization in which that power is exercised. I do not think that the decision of questions of universal interest should be submitted to those who are unable to judge of relative merit, because bad government must inevitably result from the rule of the ignorant.

If this be true, then whatever ruling influence they do exert must be for evil, for government cannot but be injured by even a slight exercise of that power which, more fully exerted could result only in ruin. This then is the general tendency. Here, in our own country, we have a practical exemplification of the truth that the rule of the ignorant will, sooner or later, result in evil. The antislavery men console themselves with the reflection that their opponents in the South are to blame for all the blood shed in our civil strife; the South says 'twas the abolitionists; while conservatives stand upon medium ground & endeavor to thrust the responsibility upon the radicalists of both sides. The truth is, in my opinion that neither abolitionist nor fireater[23] are entirely to blame, for the difficulty was with the masses themselves. 'Twas the people who placed idle wranglers in our halls of legislation & supported those whose predjudices & bad passions were the elements of discord. A close scrutiny cannot fail to show that the responsibility of our present strife lies almost entirely with the mass of uneducated voters—men who exercised the privilege of the elective franchise without even a knowledge of its meaning. It needs no remarkable vision to see this when we know that the foreign vote of this country has become a miserable tool, which, falling into the hands of unprincipled politicians is used only for evil. These facts induce the belief that the tendency of Universal Suffrage is evil.

The legitimate object of government is the greatest possible good to the greatest possible number. Anything obstructing this object is, of course, detrimental to the common interest. Now, Univ. Suff. places power in the hands of ignorance & vice; & just in proportion as this power is exercised must civilization & intelligence suffer. Here, then, the matter stands:—an evil obstructs the workings of an institution whose only legitimate object is good—the removal of that evil is demanded by both justice & expediency,—but through the jealousy & predjudice of the ignorant, the wrong receives support. The earnest & virtuous *worker,* who has acquired wealth & position, & who deserves higher privileges than the ignorant & vicious idler, is debarred the enjoyments justly accruing to him because those who cannot sympathize in his feelings are numerous & powerful enough to make their evil influence felt. Should true justice be thus violated, for the vindication of the false? If the man of progress does not receive higher privileges, proportionate to his advancement, then where is the stimulus to exertion. It is unfortunate that this idea of personal equality has become so deeply rooted as to render unpredjudiced scrutiny almost impossible:—unfortunate, I say, because it retards the development of those sentiments, which, sooner or later must result in the established supremacy of the educated. I have been tempted to branch out upon this subject because it seems to me to be a striking illustration of the short-sightedness of popular opinion. If the subject has *bored* you, I am entirely willing to be held responsible; & you may, if you can, "return it with interest compounded."

Your views & mine differ very essentially upon the subject of a Deity. I can perceive within myself no feeling which would permit me to regard a difficulty as satisfactorily explained, when the explanation involved the whole matter in even greater darkness than before. You say that you have no sympathy with "those philosophers like the author of your cat & mouse proposition, who are continu-

23. The term used to describe the most ardent Southern secessionists.

ally endeavoring to quarrel with God on account of his mistakes in creating the Universe." Upon this matter my opinions are very decided, & my sympathies just opposite to your own. If I even accepted the idea of a Supreme Being, I could regard him only with hate & contempt. In my opinion, this world, as created by a God, is nothing more nor less than a stigma upon, a disgrace to its creator. It is the most gigantic—the most absurd failure possible. I dont attack the idea of "Death a blessing": there, we agree. But I cannot but detest a being who would make make [*sic*] natural laws, the working of which would destroy the happiness of his creatures.

If we confine the question to what is generally regarded as the workings of nature, even then, your assertion, or rather opinion that "pain mentally, morally, & physically is simply corrective," cannot stand for a moment. Who is responsible for the pain of a death by lightning, by flood, the freezing of the impoverished, etc., etc.? If pain is simply corrective then why pain in death; since you think that to be the end of man, how can you regard it as corrective? Suppose it teaches others to avoid the course which led him to occupy such a position, that is, suppose the pain in one man is "corrective for others,["] is not justice violated? Besides, the most virtuous often die the most painful deaths. No, Sam, I cannot agree with you that "wrong & pain are cause & effect." To me, such an idea is indeed a cruel one. I differ with most of people in thinking that to acknowledge a Supreme Power is to make the unnatural impossible. When God rules & directs it seems to me that everything must move in obedience to his will. The idea of an opposing power is simply absurd, for if omnipotence willed all else could be flung in an instant from existence. If I have an evil tendency, it was implanted by God. If I kill my fellow, I was influenced by God so to do. In short my every action, wish, thought, mental, moral, & physical effort can be traced to no other source than the first great cause which I would have accepted.

Nor could it be confined to the individual. If two nations war upon eachother, the God who rules supreme is alone responsible. All the bad passions which influence the component parts on both sides were implanted & fostered by him; every blow struck, he directs; for all the evil resulting he & he alone is responsible. You will say that it was all caused by man's evil nature. But I claim that we can accept God only as a first cause: & not a first cause of good alone, but of all that results from existence. I do not think myself powerful enough to violate God's commandment when I thereby cross his will. If I do wrong it is with the knowledge & permission of the *most high;* else, all action were impossible. With these facts so clear, I cannot accept the idea of a Deity. Nature instead of being well arranged, is, to me, a most miserable confusion, & could reflect nothing but disgrace upon a creator. In fact, the only *natural* feeling that I could have for

Fig. 24. Ashenfelter's sister,
Hannah Ashenfelter Laning.
(Courtesy of Pennypacker
Mills, County of Montgomery,
Schwenksville, PA)

such a being is, as I have said,—a hate, & that the most bitter & intense possible.
So, I reject all such an idea, & accept the present, the world, just as I find it, & ask
no impertinant questions.

March. 1865.

I finished the above on last Friday & started the next morning for Phoenixville to attend Sister's wedding.[24] I had intended to tell you of my intention so to
do, but did not know exactly when the event was to take place until just before I
started. I arrived in Phoenixville Saturday, the 25th. & the same evening called
on Annie. We had an uninterrupted conversation of several hours duration
with the purport of which I am afraid David would not be particularly well
pleased, were he posted. I wish to say here that, if I ever marry, it will be only
after I have risen to a position which I would be willing for my wife to occupy.
Annie knows this & accepts the knowledge with a quiet smile. I expressed to
her the intention which I had entertained of presenting the matter to her Father's consideration. She said there was no use in so doing. It would only make

24. SMA's sister Hannah married Isaac Laning on February 28, 1865. They eventually
moved to Bridgeton, New Jersey, and had four children.

her position more unpleasant without helping matters in the least. I think that both Mr. & Mrs Euen will live to regret their course: they certainly will if I can do anything in that direction. I called on her again Tuesday evening. When I entered the parlor Mrs. Euen retired with an almost inaudible ["]good evening["] & exceedingly distant manner,—& I—swallowed my offended pride & laughed internally, feeling relieved & grateful for the time. It is develish galling though, to feel that you are not welcome, & I have made up my mind to trouble them with my presence just as seldom as possible. I have also resolved to repay them at my earliest opportunity[.]

I received yours of the 19th. ult. &, believe me, the mood in which it was written is one with which I can fully sympathize. I often experience precisely the same feelings & have the same longing for some one into whose ears I can pour even my most secret thoughts. A confidant is, as you may have observed, almost a necessity with me,—so much so that I frequently violate my ideas of policy & put in writing that which I would very much prefer to communicate orally. But what, in the name of Misery, induced you to draw upon your imagination for so doleful a picture as that which occupied the second page of your letter. You must feel lonely indeed when you allow such thoughts to gain the supremacy. I received your invitation to attend the Bancroft's "Public."[25] Many thanks, but cant come. However, I believe the time is already past. I also acknowledge the receipt of $0.15[.]

I say, blow the *irony*,—a week ago it would have been d—n —& all connected therewith;—comments, criticisms, internal & external, wasted paper, &c. &c. &c. etc. Away with them all, & let us touch upon literature for awhile. While you read what follows, I dont want you to imagine that your most humble is the author. I wanted a copy of it at the same time that [I wanted][26] you to see it; so I just enclosed it here. Tell me when you reply what you think of

Composition No.2.

By

J. W. Jackson

I enclose also a copy of "Demon Despair."[27] When Jackson wrote it, he thought seriously of committing suicide. The poem depicts his struggle of mind. The scene is at the grave of a departed mistress.

25. According to his autobiography, SWP joined the Bancroft Literary Society in 1864. The society named itself after the famous historian George Bancroft because he had donated a set of his works to the organization.

26. SMA inserted a quotation mark beneath the previous "I wanted," to signify that he meant to use the same words again here.

27. This enclosure is no longer in the collection at PM.

Please return the Essay & Poem when you reply to this rambling epistle.
Your Friend,
Sing Ashenfelter.

Wasted Paper
  At Your Service
Chum Sends Regards

Dickinson College
Mar. 5, 1865

Dear Sam,

When I was in Phoenixville a few days since, Hal told me that you thought of changing your boarding house, & might do so, at any time. I have a letter written[28] but hesitate to send it to 433 [Chestnut Street][29] until I hear from you. I will risk this, but not that. Let me know as soon as possible in order that I may forward.

Your Friend
Sing Ashenfelter

Dickinson College
March 30. 1865

Dear Sam,

I sit down to write to you because I have nothing else in particular to occupy my attention, & because I have caught myself wondering at your silence. Graduation is drawing nigh & I am very much rejoiced thereat. I am beginning to find College restraint exceedingly irksome: the old feeling of discontent with settled life & routine becomes so strong, at times, as almost to escape control. I am impatient for a struggle, a contest with active life, anything in fact that will arouse me & make exertion a necessity. You know, I was a loafer at school;—& I have been nothing more throughout my College course. Were I to take the trouble to make an estimate, I am of [the] opinion that I would find my amount of study per day does not exceed what could be well performed in fifteen or twenty min-

28. This probably refers to the previous letter, which SMA began in February and concluded in March.

29. Beginning in the fall of 1863, SWP stayed with his uncle Joseph R. Whitaker (1824–95) at Mary Whitehead's boardinghouse at 433 Chestnut Street in Philadelphia.

utes. I usually glance at the first page or two of my text books, & through [throw] them aside with an impatient bored feeling indicative of anything rather than a proper degree of interest. By good luck, rather than good management, I keep up with the class, & my farce of mental culture goes on. However these are feelings with which you are never afflicted, or at least never allow to predominate, & so I will discontinue the recital.

I have no settled plan of action subsequent to my becoming an A.B.—humbug—To tell the truth, it would not be characteristic if I had. I feel very much like taking no active measures & "waiting for something to turn up." If I could manage to do something absurd, or cursedly foolish, I suppose the majority of my humors & inclinations would be gratified. One thing is certain:—I will make an existance for myself, or starve. I sometimes feel as though it were a matter of much rejoicing that my parents are not blessed with a surplus of this worlds goods, for the fact may save their son from becoming a confirmed loafer—a miserable do-nothing[.] If I expressed the wish, I presume Father would pay my expenses as a law-student: but he never shall. I may spend the summer in Phoenixville, but beyond that, he shall never expend one cent on my account. So for the present, you see, law is out of the question: for I must first have the money. My idea is in a certain manner protective too; for if I were to attempt to study the profession in my present prevalent humor, I feel that it would never amount to anything. *I must have a stirring up.*

Your Friend,
Sing Ashenfelter.

Dickinson College
Apr. 3, 1865.

Dear Sam,

In reply to yours of the 1st., I can only quote:
"Who's sold? I declare by Jupiter, Pluto & all the saints in the heathen calendar that it isn't me."

Your Friend
Sing Ashenfelter

Dickinson College
Apr. 9. 1865

Dear Sam,

I was looking over some old papers, an hour or so since, & lit upon the enclosed.[30] Some years hence, I might not wish to mar pleasant retrospect by meeting with it again, so, I return it. If the document is of no particular use, I advise you burn it.

Hoping soon to hear from you,

Your Friend,

Sing Ashenfelter.

Dickinson College

Apr. 24. 1865

Dear Sam,

I have just had perpetrated upon me what I would call an infernal piece of impudence. Lloyd has had the audacity to send me an *Independent Phoenix* containing a notice of his marriage.[31] Deceit I could have borne, silence I would not have murmured against, but anything so evidently indicative of the depreciated estimation in which I am held completely oversets me. I know not whether to laugh or curse. I acknowledged the receipt of the paper in a note of six lines; informing the youth that I was surprised that he should have seen proper to send even so slight a notice of the event. It is my intention to take advantage of the first opportunity of asking him what remuneration would be sufficient to induce him to go to the devil. In my opinion, he is a little bit ashamed of having made such a fool of himself. He has taken the step with his eyes wide open & he cannot but have seen his own folly;—if any disagreeable consequences ensue, he is deserving of them.

You ask as to whether I gained my impressions of a difference between you two from observation alone, or from more substantial grounds. From a remark which I heard him make, as to one of your letters. It was something above four pages in length, &, after disserting upon the *humbug* of long letters, said something to the effect that he would not trouble himself to reply. When I left home last vacation I asked him which of us owed the other a letter. He believed he was indebted to me to that extent & would write soon. I have never heard from him. In my opinion he has intended to take this last step for some time, & discontinued corresponding with us because he could not persuade himself to take us into confidence. Lide told sister Emmie that they had been engaged for but one month. I dont know whether Mrs. Lloyd told the truth or not, but if she did, she was a fool for doing so.

30. This is no longer in the collection at PM.
31. Horace Lloyd married Mary Eliza Vanderslice on April 11, 1865.

I have considered well what you have said as to my future & have concluded to enter upon the study of law immediately after graduation. I must however adhere to my determination to accept no aid from Father, who is, I believe, willing to assist me during my term of study:—so I am "in search of a place" "looking for something to turn up" &c. &c. If anything desirable comes under your notice, let me know; for I will study in the city, if possible. I told Doc. Johnson that if he heard of anything in the city by which I could support myself, he would do me a favor by letting me know of the same. All of which he promised to do.

The dinner bell rings, & I close.

Your Friend

Sing Ashenfelter

P.S. I have changed my mind & simply written & told Lloyd that he has my best wishes.

Idem

Dickinson College

May 9. 1865

Dear Sam,

This is the Twenty-first anniversary of the day upon which I was unfortunate enough to be born. I am an American Citizen; & feel big because of the proud consciousness that I have the ability to neutralize the vote of the most rampant copperhead, or paddy,[32] America can boast of.[33] To quote from the late, lamented, Lloyd, "I feel like a bob-tailed pullet on a rickety hen-roost,"[34] & could crow "like all tarnation." And just here, with this new dignity fresh upon me, I wish to correct an erroneous impression into which you have fallen. I did *not* learn, through the Post Office, that letters were passing between Alice Lee & yourself, & was not at the end of my rope when that conclusion had been arrived at. For instance, I discovered, inadvertently, that one of your letters extended to the length of seven pages. I say inadvertently because the predominant feeling in me was that I had no right to know more than just what you

32. "Paddy" was an epithet for Irish Americans, most of whom were Democrats and also considered Copperheads.

33. SMA's reflections upon turning twenty-one reflect the views of many young men of that time toward this milestone birthday. See Jon Grinspan, "A Birthday Like None Other: Turning Twenty-One in the Age of Popular Politics," in *Age in America: The Colonial Era to the Present*, ed. Corinne T. Field and Nicholas L. Syrett (New York: New York Univ. Press, 2015), 86–99.

34. A bobtailed animal has a short tail; a pullet is a young hen.

chose to reveal; & although I always had a slight curiosity upon the subject, I yet never attempted anything like an investigation. However, I am willing to drop this subject, as such seems to be your wish. Take care that you never suffer from an analogous but more enduring sentiment. I speak as one having knowledge. While I think of it, how about that champagne supper promised by Lloyd the late, lamented, to Andy. I heard the promise made, &, although I drink not of the poison whence cometh intoxication, would yet like to be present when it has its redemption.

Jackson acknowledges that the error was his in,

> "Quits the earth for joy or misery
> Joy or bliss forever more"

And pitches into me for submitting his composition to anyone, previous to a revision. The poem as I told you was written some years since, & is not, by any means, to be taken as an index of Jackson's present ability. If I could induce him to keep sober, I do not think I exaggerate in saying that the literary world would be startled next fall by the appearance of a new star. He has a work half finished which I really regard as one of the finest things ever written by an American. This is in confidence, as I am the only one to whom Jack has confided this information, & he intends to publish anonymously. You were right in that surmise as to those few lines being in imitation of Longfellow: Jack thinks that even he has his good points:—although he is bitter in his condemnation of Hyperion, Evangeline, & Excelsior.[35] But Poe is his favorite of American authors;—as Shelley[36] & Byron[37] of English. The former he is almost a second edition of. I have known him to sit down & compose metrically, with as much facility as others, prose; but he is so erratic that he frequently will not touch his pen for weeks at a time. I have been wanting him to write some half-dozen lines for me now fully three weeks, but I have not obtained them yet, & cannot until [he] is in a writing

---

35. Longfellow published "Hyperion" and "Excelsior" in 1839 and 1841, respectively. Jackson seems to have been in the minority in his assessment of the poem "Evangeline," which received broad critical acclaim soon after its publication in 1847 and is now regarded as one of Longfellow's greatest works.

36. Probably the English poet Percy Bysshe Shelley (1792–1822), although this may refer to his wife, Mary Shelley (1797–1851), the English writer best known for her 1818 novel *Frankenstein*.

37. George Gordon Byron, or "Lord Byron" (1788–1824), was an English politician more famous for his poetry than his statesmanship.

humor. I have only the consolation of knowing that they will be the first things on hand when he does commence to write.

You say "Bully for Grant. Hip! Hip!" Cant see it, for I think the problem to have been capable of a much more favorable solution. About the time you wrote that letter I was cursing Abraham Lincoln for his leniency. I dont like the terms upon which the rebel armies have surrendered. I dont think it brave or generous, having accepted such terms, to come in with afterclap severity. I do not think that rebels should have ever had the permission to return unmolested to their homes; but, when the permission had been granted, it was indeed contemptible to place thereon the forced construction of our Attorney General Speed, or the restrictions of Genl. Halleck. It would have pleased me better to have had Grant retain his prestige of "Unconditional Surrender" as his sobriquet.[38]

I repeat, Miss Sue & I understand eachother but Lloyd & Lide dont. I am of the same opinion still.

Your Friend
Sing Ashenfelter

Dickinson College
May. 14. 1865

Dear Sam,

Yours of the 11th came duly to hand & replying thereto is the only occupation on hand this Sunday morning. I have not, of course, communicated to anyone the fact that you are "in ile," & should have refrained from so doing even had you not requested me to.

---

38. Union general Ulysses S. Grant had become famous for demanding the "unconditional surrender" of Vicksburg in the summer of 1863. When Confederate general Robert E. Lee surrendered the Army of Northern Virginia to him on April 9, 1865, however, Grant gave very generous terms, permitting "each officer and man . . . to return to their homes, not to be disturbed by United States authority so long as they observe their parole and the laws in force where they reside." In an official opinion dated April 22, Attorney General James Speed (1812–87) stated that Grant did not have authority to permit Confederates to return to Washington, DC, or to the loyal states: "The officers and soldiers of General Lee's army, then, who had homes prior to the rebellion in the northern States, took up their residences within the rebel States and abandoned their homes in the loyal States, and when General Grant gave permission to them, by the stipulation, to return to their homes, it cannot be understood as a permission to return to any part of the loyal States." Federal authorities around this time stationed Maj. Gen. Henry Wager Halleck (1815–72) in Richmond, placing him in command of the Military Division of the James, because they believed that he would not be so lenient toward the former Confederates.

However, what little likelyhood of a thoughtless allusion to the subject did exist is now entirely dissipated. I wish to repeat a remark made in my last—I speak as one having *knowledge*. I was not aware that I had made any quotation, & if you will refer to my letter, I think you will find the remark to be destitute of the peculiar characters which always indicate such intention. Can you conceive of such a thing as an imitation? You quote "he spake, not as the scribes & Pharisees, but as one having authority." I would most respectfully suggest, as Matthew's comment upon Christ's sermon on the mount; "For he *taught* them as one having authority, & not as the scribes." Matt. VII-29. And just here, with your remarks on that bit of advice I gave fresh upon my mind, I wish to say that I feel more confidant than ever that the five dollars, pending an event in my life, will fall into my hands.

Jackson thinks that it is a great pity that Tennyson was not fortunate enough to die immediately after writing "In Memoriam": his subsequent publications having been almost sufficient to destroy whatever good opinion *its* merits may have aroused. His comment upon Enoch Arden[39] was, "it's a cursed shame to spoil a poet, by making him *Laureate:* for Tennyson might have amounted to something, if he had been left alone.["][40] Maud,[41] he says, is a disgrace to the author, & an insult to the public—the first, because it is incomprehensible nonsense; the last, because its publication presupposes fools enough to make the sale profitable.

Giving Jackson's opinion reminds me of the fact that I had entertained the intention of adding a little of his latest experience thereto. He was dismissed from College on the 10th. inst. For the last month, the students have been the source of considerable annoyance to the good people of Carlisle. Sometime since, two of them—the students—in a drunken frolic, tore down a national ensign which was attached to the house of the Episcopal Minister. They were detected, brought before a magistrate & bound over to appear at court. One of them has since departed for lands unknown. After the excitement of that affair had partially abated, a crowd of drunken students resisted an attempt at arrest, made by the town authorities, & one of them drew a knife upon the Chief-Burgess. They were identified, had a hearing, & were placed under bail to appear at next court.[42] The latter

---

39. English poet Alfred, Lord Tennyson (1809–92) published "Enoch Arden" in 1864 and "In Memoriam A.H.H." in 1849. He wrote the latter about his close friend from Cambridge, Arthur Henry Hallam, who had died unexpectedly in 1833.

40. In 1850 Queen Victoria appointed Tennyson poet laureate of Great Britain and Ireland.

41. Tennyson published "Maud" in 1855.

42. SMA's account of Dickinson students' shenanigans in Carlisle may have been an exception to the norm. Historian Julie A. Mujic notes that, by and large, colleges and towns had a "symbiotic relationship" during the war years, gleaning from their relationship "common

is just the party I would have been with had I not stopped drinking. These occurrences had the effect of making the Faculty very energetic in enforcing College law: four students were dismissed & Jackson, although he was not engaged in either difficulty, yet because of his loose habits, was one of the number.[43] About fifty of the students formed a procession & escorted Jack. to the depot: very much to the disgust of our President & Faculty. More of Jackson anon.

As the classes reassemble three years after graduation to take their second degrees, it is customary to elect a President to each just before the termination of their College course—to which position your most obediant was, a few days since, unanimously elected—excepting, of course, his own vote.

Before I had half-finished reading your account of the remarkable church services which you attended, I had given internal expression to the wish to have been with you: so your request that I would pardon you for entertaining the same wish was entirely unnecessary. Of course I need not tell you that I endorse fully your sentiments upon the subject of squeamishness.

Now, for a question or two. Judging from your own experience, how much will a law-course in the city cost? Will it be possible for me to enter the same office with yourself: &, if so, upon what terms? If I cannot obtain a situation in the city, do you think it would be advisable for me to borrow the money for a law-course?—i.e. if it is possible for me so to do?

If you feel any reluctance in answering these questions, do not hesitate to tell me so. Write when convenient.

Your Friend

Sing Ashenfelter

P.S. Will you oblige me by investing two or three dollars in a ladies' pen-knife: & forwarding the same, by mail, at your earliest convenience? A knife with not more than two or three blades, if possible.

Idem.

---

strength, protection, and escape from their worldly concerns." See Mujic, "Between Campus and War: Students, Patriotism, and Education at Midwestern Universities during the American Civil War" (PhD diss., Kent State Univ., 2012), 22.

43. According to the Faculty Minutes, Jackson had been absent from class a good deal in late 1864 and early 1865. On April 3, 1865, the minutes state: "It was moved that Jackson be advised to leave on account of his minus marks and habits of drinking." They record on May 15: "[Pulaski] Melick and Jackson were reported as having been cut off by minus marks, and habits of drinking. [Howard] Hodson & [George W. G.] Thompson were privately sent away for habits, drinking and neglect of duty."

May 15.

I received yours this morning & I write to tell you that I am as blue as the devil, & that the quotation to which you alluded was taken from Byron's Manfred.[44]

I most emphatically endorse the old song,

"For men must work, & women must weep;

And the sooner it's over, the sooner to sleep."[45]

Your Friend

Sing Ashenfelter

Dickinson College

May 19. 1865

Dear Sam,

Your letter, with knife enclosed, was received this morning, & time being abundant, I make immediate acknowledgement thereof. The purchase was eminently satisfactory—so much so that I almost feel tempted to bore you with thanks. I have often thought while watching Jackson in his culinary operations that to board one's self was the only truly independent mode of living. The more I saw of it, the better I liked it, &, here at College, I went as far as my position would allow toward the gratification of my wishes upon the subject. No one supposes that I have any scarcity of means—in truth, Father is quite liberal—& had I undertaken to board myself, the act would have been attributed to no other motive than that of meaness. Hence, I was compelled to do the next best thing; i.e. join a boarding club. There were two in existence here, but neither suited me; & so, communicating my ideas to one of the most popular of my fellow-students, I induced him to join in my effort, & together, we established The Continental Club of Dickinson, which I am happy to say, furnishes an excellent table to sixteen of the best fellows in College,—self-excluded—at the moderate rate of three dollars & sixty cents per week. I write at length upon this subject merely to show you that if you are prevented from renting a room & living a free life only by the want of a companion, I would be happy to render such a want *null & void* if *you* are willing. It is strange, but the very morning of the receipt of your letter containing the first allusion to Burton,[46] I was occupied in

44. Lord Byron, "Manfred: A Dramatic Poem" (1817).

45. Charles Kingsley, "Three Fishers" (1851). This poem tells of the grief endured by the families of three fishermen who perished in a storm.

46. Robert Burton (1577–1640), a scholar at Oxford University, published *The Anatomy of Melancholy* in 1621.

wondering what the Character of his Anatomy *was*. An undeniable instance of *animal magnetism*[.][47]

I am engaged at present upon Leigh Hunt's "Dante & his Genius,"[48] which depreciates—justly—the former & exalts the latter. I purpose finishing the Italian Poets previous to taking another metaphysical dive—in which line the next on my list is Draper's Intellectual Development of Europe,[49] which Dr. Johnson thinks every man should leave untouched until his intellect is in its prime. By the by, the Dr. recommended to the consideration of our class, a few days since, Buckel's History of Civilization.[50] Have you read it? He seemed to think it necessary to qualify his recommendation with a caution against allowing its fallacies to have too much weight.

I have determined that when I come to the City I will begin to do what has not very prominently characterized my course at Dickinson. Here my position has not been so much that of a good *student*, as of a good *fellow*—remember, I would make this statement to no one else—& while my social position in College has ever been enviable, my scholarship, as indicated by class standing, has been very low. In my Sophomore year, I stood fifth in a class of twenty-two.—In my Junior Year, fifteenth in a class of sixteen, of whom *one* took no standing whatever. Prof. Hillman—my patron—said to me one day last session, "Ashenfelter you are doing injustice to every student in College who can be at all influenced by the actions of another. You are popular, are considered by most of the students to be the most able man in your class, & yet, your carelessness & indifference to study are—I was about to say notorious[.] If you go through your course without study others will think that they ought to be able to do the same, & swamp their education in attempting it." These were, as nearly as I can remember, the words the Prof. used, & I never failed again, in ———— *his room*[.] However, I am glad that the end is near, & although I will be sorry to part with my many Carlisle friends, yet this life of a loafer has become so detestable that, were this the close of my Junior Year, I would never stay to take my Diploma.

47. "Animal magnetism" was a concept developed by eighteenth-century German physician Franz Anton Mesmer, which identified an invisible and mysterious force capable of inducing hypnosis. The term came to refer more generally to one's charisma or charm.

48. James Henry Leigh Hunt (1784–1859) was an English poet and writer. SMA is likely alluding to his essay "Dante: Critical Notice of His Life and Genius," in Leigh Hunt, *Stories from the Italian Poets: With Lives of the Writers*, 2 vols. (London: Chapman and Hall, 1846), 1:1–77.

49. John William Draper, *A History of the Intellectual Development of Europe*, 2 vols. (1863; repr., London: George Bell and Sons, 1875).

50. Henry Thomas Buckle, *History of Civilization in England*, 2 vols. (London: Parker, Son, and Bourn, 1857, 1861).

Fig. 25. Prof. Samuel D. Hillman, ca. 1865. (Courtesy of Archives and Special Collections, Dickinson College, Carlisle, PA)

The Honor Man of our class asked me to-day to review & suggest corrections to his address. The members of the Faculty will not touch any of our speeches to amend them, & Reid,[51] who is a hard-working digger at text books, came to me. At first, I most positively declined, for, to tell the truth, I felt unequal to the task. I afterwards reconsidered the matter, however, & concluded that if I did no good, I would, at any rate do no harm; for Reid, who is a fellow of considerable ability, writes with most excellent ideas, a remarkably awkward construction. I have not as yet told him that I have concluded to do as he wishes. Now, the narration of all this indicates considerable vanity; &, to tell what my real feelings were, the circumstance has made me quite self congratulatory: But *you know* that to you alone would they be written or spoken, & *you* already know of my weaknesses. Enclosed is the price of [the] knife. I would be very happy to have a description of Mr. McCall,[52] etc.

Your Friend,

Sing Ashenfelter

51. Charles Wesley Reid of West Chester, Pennsylvania, a member of the class of 1865, won the gold medal for oratory and the prize in logic in June 1864. On June 27, 1865, he won the first prize in mathematics. Reid delivered the valedictory address at the commencement ceremony on June 29.

52. Peter McCall (1809–80), a prominent Democrat in Philadelphia, served as professor of practice, pleading, and evidence in the Law Department of the University of Pennsylvania from 1852 to 1860. SWP and SMA both read law under him.

[P.S.] In explanation of the style in which this is written, I would state that I had been exercising violently previous to commencing.

Dickinson College
June. 1. 1865

Dear Sam,

Yours reached me this morning, & in reply I would say that I will congratulate myself quite heartily if I can obtain such a situation as that to which you refer. What I have been thinking of doing was, as you know, the last alternative. I could not expect Clem to recommend me upon our acquaintance alone, for that has been too limited: I have therefor written to Horace & requested him to forward to his brother a word or two relative to myself—it may be of good, it may be the reverse. As far as capabilities are concerned I have nothing to say, further than that I think a little "brushing up" would dispel whatever hesitation I might now entertain in that respect.

I would be very happy, indeed, could I obtain the situation.

Your Friend,

Sing Ashenfelter

Dickinson College.
June 6, 1865

Dear Sam,

I commenced to write to you last Sunday, but found the weather too intensely hot to admit of completing even a letter. Yesterday I sat down & wrote my graduating speech, & now I have nothing in particular to occupy my attention until Commencement. I quote from yours of May 14th. 1862—as follows, viz., "Your invitation to attend the commencement at Carlisle was rec'd to-day—& while I am much obliged to you for the kindness, I am afraid I cannot avail myself of it. I guess I will have to wait until you graduate, when I will try to be present, to see how you get along." I expect to graduate on the 29th. day of the present month, & you must endeavor to redeem your promise. I think you should at least *visit* the institution into whose care you had some idea of trusting your *mens.*[53] Now that my College course is about ended, I can look back upon it as comprising three of the happiest years it has ever been my good fortune to pass. I have never been what the Faculty would call a *good* student;—although my marks have never been

---

53. Latin for "mind."

below the *satisfactory,* & frequently reached the *exemplary.* But I do not think I exhibit undue vanity, or boast overmuch, when I say that I would not exchange places with the man who stood first in our class:—that I place a higher valuation upon my position among the students than I would upon all the honors within the gift of the Faculty. I often think that perhaps my career here will have the effect of rendering me undully vain: & internal scrutiny upon that point hardly satisfies me that such is not the case. Of course, I speak to none other as to you regarding the *ego,* & am confidant that my friends here do not regard me as very egotistical; yet I often feel as though I were generating within myself expectations above those which my abilities—be they small or great—would warrent. I trust that *the world* will bring me to sense of what powers are essential to success.

I imagine from your description that I would be well pleased with *Peter* [Mc-Call]. Political sentiments are of very little importance to me for, aside from predjudice, I would regard all party principles as coming within the same category—humbug. Regarding a knowledge of machinery as necessarily antecedent to the proper working thereof, I agree with you as to the style of office & course of study best suited to a true student. When Father was in West Chester last winter, Wayne McVeagh[54] told him that if I could make it convenient to come over sometime previous to deciding upon my course, he would like to have a conversation with me upon the subject. I will see him this summer, but think it hardly possible that he has anything to say that will materially change my plans. In a town like West Chester it would be almost impossible for me to resist my inclination for society; in the city, I think the task will be less difficult.

I expect to go to Phoenixville about the 1st of July, but *may* leave here sooner. At all events I will be home in time to *enjoy immense excitement* usually prevalent in that neighborhood on the *4th*—the *Glorious Fourth.*

As I told you, I wrote to Lloyd regarding the position which *Clem* is about to vacate. I received a letter from him yesterday stating that he had written upon the subject & would do anything within his power. Do not trouble yourself seriously about the matter, but if you hear any thing definite, let me know. I would take any position in which I could support myself & have a little spare time, rather than *borrow* the money necessary for my studies. Lloyd starts for Michigan next week on a visit to his brother.[55]

54. Wayne MacVeagh (1833–1917), a Republican politician, lawyer, and diplomat from Phoenixville, later served as attorney general under Pres. James A. Garfield.

55. Franklin Lloyd (1832–65), older brother of Horace and Clem. Frank married Rebecca Holloway in 1859 and had two children, both of whom died in infancy (1860, 1865). In a letter to SWP dated May 23, 1865, Horace expressed a desire to visit him in Michigan. Frank appears to have come back to Pennsylvania for a visit later that summer. See SMA to SWP, July

Enclosed I forward my latest *carte*. What think you?

Your Friend,

Sing Ashenfelter

P.S. The title of my Commencement Oration is "A plea for Anarchy" & therein, I borrow a sentence from one of your letters, "The great theory is that, each individual consents to give up certain of his natural rights for the good of the whole, etc. but this is only theory—&c."

Dickinson College

June 20, 1865.

Dear Sam,

I imagine I could preach quite a lengthy sermon upon the evils of procrastination;—but the *"fearful example"* is too convenient for comfort, & I will refrain. There is no denying the fact that the weather here is the reverse of stimulating, & further, that in consequence thereof, your most obedient is, well, lazy. Say such a mood occupies three-fourths of my waking hours;—the remaining fourth is hardly more than sufficient for the completion of my *arrangements* for departure from Carlisle. All of which above is intended as a substitute for promptness in replying to your last letter.

There is considerable variety of opinion relative to my *Carte.*—Comments are somewhat as follows—"Splendid Picture," "Coming out of the Cellar," "Very Good[,]" "In the Pit," & "Somewhat Theatrical," &c. "O wad some power, &c[.]"[56] What do you think of the enclosed?

Is there anything surprising in the fact that I have my last letters so arranged as to make reference thereto convenient? I have lately read over & arranged all your letters, & enjoyed several hearty laugh[s] over ideas of mine, in the past, which you had set yourself to controverting. I imagine I must have written some exceedingly foolish letters. You need not feel at all flattered by the fact of my having added one of your sentences to that humbug—commencement oration. Believe me, your idea could have been thrown into better company. Spare me further sarcasm on the subject of penmanship. Sometimes I am almost inclined to imagine that the interpretation placed upon your expression of countenance & conversational style, by a certain young lady, is a true one. It would certainly seem so, at first glance.

22, 1865. He died from congestion of the lungs on October 7, 1865, in Bangor, Michigan, and was brought back to Philadelphia for burial.

56. This is an allusion to Robert Burns's 1786 poem, "To a Louse."

This letter was started on a full sheet, but sunshine & flies have been sufficient to confine it to a single leaf.

Your Friend

Sing Ashenfelter

Phoenixville

July 22, 1865

Dear Sam,

I am sitting here, at home, nursing a sore toe, &,—it having occurred to me that I was indebted to you to the extent of one letter,—endeavoring to improve my time with pen, ink, & this sheet of thesis-paper; it being the only one convenient. I think I will be prepared to return to the city with you after your sojourn in Phoenixville. Wayne McVeagh had nothing to advance excepting a little gratuitous &, I presume, excellent advice. He commended my plan of studying in the city, & more than intimated that his success was very greatly owing to certain favorable circumstances. He said that a country lawyer in the Eastern or Middle States might work himself forward, but the chances were very much against him. He advised "most emphatically" study in the city, &, if you have a very good opening, practice there; otherwise, go South or West. I did not attach much weight to his advice except from the fact that it coincided with my own previous opinions. He very kindly offered to do all in his power to obtain me a situation when I alluded to the fact that I was desirous of working my own way through. He said "If you meet with anything, let me know, & I will come to the city & do my best to secure it for you."

Well, I have been reading some little of the law. I began Blackstone a day or two since & have read the first fifty or sixty pages.[57] I do not find it as dry as I had anticipated. I know not how it may be with most of beginners, but, with me, a feeling of awkwardness accompanies every effort. I feel very much as though I had taken hold of something almost unimaginable & would give the world to know just how to deal with it.

Ben & I usually employ our evenings in loafing, walking, smoking, or playing cards. Franklin has departed for *Lancaster City* on a visit, & we are left alone in our glory. Andy came down last Saturday but returned again on Sunday: so that, with the exception of Saturday evening, I saw but little of him. Ben & I

---

57. William Blackstone (1723–80) was an eighteenth-century English jurist whose four-volume treatise *Commentaries on the Laws of England* (1765–69) was required reading for law students during the nineteenth century.

called on Lloyd & Lide a few evenings since & enjoyed at least a partial view of some of the joys of married life. The young man is certainly very attentive, anticipating every little wish—& all that. I dont know whether he has noticed it, but I have never offered my congratulations; if he has, I hope he will attribute my failure to do so to the true cause—none to offer.

I waited until the five o'clock train on Saturday &—served me right—was most beautifully sold. The young lady took her departure an hour or so earlier.

Having nothing more to say on particular topics, & any thing general being entirely out of the question, I subside[.]

Your Friend

Sing Ashenfelter.

EPILOGUE

Postwar Romances

THOUGHTS OF ANNIE EUEN PREOCCUPIED ASHENFELTER'S MIND FOR AT least six years after he graduated from Dickinson, and for much of that time he felt like he was drifting aimlessly. "I feel that I lack stability, that I lack purpose," he wrote to Pennypacker in September 1866. "It is a knowledge of this that has had much to do with my actions towards Annie. I love the girl with the strongest love of which I am capable." Yet Ashenfelter was wary of pursuing a long-term commitment with her because he doubted that he would ever be financially independent enough to marry her. "To have kept Annie waiting all these years, waiting on an uncertainty, would not have been right," he lamented. He also knew that his motives had not been entirely "magnanimous" and pure. "There was considerable selfishness at the bottom of my desire to break these ties." He evidently had a "longing" to move away from Phoenixville and took "advantage of the first opportunity of gratifying it."

In 1866 Ashenfelter moved to Salem, New Jersey, where he became editor of the *National Standard*. While he appears to have been initially happy there, he soon became despondent, feeling "much dissatisfied as ever I was" and finding little "in life worth the trouble of living for." Ashenfelter contemplated suicide but knew that he could not take such a drastic action while his parents were still alive. Instead, he decided that his "object in life" would be "to make the best of it" and that he would "gratify" his "longing" to see more of the world. He informed Pennypacker that he would soon "commence to 'Drift' in earnest."[1] And drift he did. In late 1866 Ashenfelter began an almost two-year sojourn in

1. SMA to SWP, Sept. 23, 1866, PM.

South America. Then in 1868 he settled in Rock Island, Illinois, where he concluded his study of law. From there he moved to New Mexico Territory in 1870.

Before setting out on these adventures, "an impulse" led Ashenfelter to propose to Annie. She turned him down, which apparently caused him to leave behind an "unkind letter" to her when he departed. For years Annie's name made regular appearances in Ashenfelter's letters, but her memory did not stop him from pursuing other amorous conquests along the way. In 1871 he asked Pennypacker how Annie was doing but then added that "if she but knew how often I have been in love, since then, she would conclude she took the wisest step of her life" in turning him down.[2]

He was not exaggerating. Ashenfelter's adventures abroad and out West brought a slew of new romantic interests. In 1868 he told Pennypacker about "a poor little girl" whom he had impregnated and "deserted" a year earlier in South America. Ostensibly bucking the racial prejudices of his day, Ashenfelter exclaimed that if she were there with him in New Mexico, he would marry her "and let people talk as they pleased." He then revealed to his old friend: "She has given birth to a boy &, confound her eyes, she has named him *Singleton*. What do you think of that—Singleton Villamil." When Pennypacker told him that another girl from home had been in love with him, Ashenfelter replied: "Confound it! Is a fellow to suppose that every young lady whose waist he encircles is in love with me?"[3]

Then there was Mary, a girl in New Mexico whom Ashenfelter described as "young—only fifteen, very pretty. Regular features—glorious eyes. Hits plumb center with rifle or pistol. Rides like a witch. Deliciously ignorant. Blushes beautifully. Plays the harp and all that & is going to the states to be educated—much against her own will." Ashenfelter was "captured" by Mary's pluck and courage, writing that "she's been in several indian fights and used her pistol with the rest." On horseback she had no equal. "Her horse ran off with her a day or two before I came down here, and instead of getting frightened & loseing control of him she rode him straight for the river & brought him to his senses with a good ducking. . . . In short she's all that's brave and daring and yet as shy, modest, and womanly as one could wish." Ashenfelter's infatuation was complete. Evidently, Mary was "a darned sight prettier than Annie (or Anna) or Laura or Sue or any of those"

2. SMA to SWP, Aug. 12, 1867, July 24, 1868, and May 31, 1871, PM.

3. SMA to SWP, Oct. 26, 1868, PM. In 1880 SMA's wife wrote to SWP, "Sing is drinking again, and in his drunken talk, he has told me that he has a child in South America and that you know about it. Will you please write to me giving all the information you can, in regard to the matter." See Nettie Ashenfelter to SWP, Oct. 13, 1880, PM.

Fig. 26. Samuel W. Pennypacker in old age. (Courtesy of the Library of Congress)

Left: Fig. 27. Singleton M. Ashenfelter in old age. (From *Genealogical History of the Cassel Family*, 1896) *Right*: Fig. 28. Nettie Bennett Ashenfelter in old age. (From *Daughters of the American Revolution Magazine*, 1917)

other girls back in Pennsylvania. "I'm quite in love with her," he wrote wryly, "for the present at any rate. Those things are but transient with me, you know."[4]

Transient indeed. As he predicted, his attractions soon shifted to another woman in New Mexico—now, it seemed, for the final time. In 1872 he met the niece of Col. J. Y. Bennett, who was kind enough to give him lodging. The niece, Jennett "Nettie" Bennett, had been engaged to a soldier since she was fifteen. Ashenfelter nevertheless flirted with her instantly, and the knowledge of her longstanding engagement "merely served to add to the interest of the sur-roundings." Now twenty-eight years old, he was concerned that he was "rapidly becoming fixed in my old habits" and "needed some sort of change—needed a wife." Resolving to win Nettie, he did perhaps the most Ashenfelter-esque thing he ever did:

> One evening I quietly asked her to marry me. "You know of my engagement Mr. Ashenfelter?" Answered affirmatively. "Then what could you expect me to say to a proposition such as you have made?" "I expect you, Nettie, to write east and ask to be released from your engagement, because you love me better than all the world; and then, Nettie, I expect you to marry me."

He concluded the story, "It took *cheek,* Pen, my boy, but I got away with it."[5]

4. SMA to SWP, May 31, 1871, PM.
5. SMA to SWP, Sept. 19, Oct. 31, 1872, PM.

Curriculum at Dickinson College

BELOW IS THE COURSE OF STUDY FOR EACH OF ASHENFELTER'S YEARS AT Dickinson College. The lists for each academic year are from the edition of the *Catalogue of Dickinson College* applicable for when Ashenfelter stood in that class.

Freshman Course of Study (1861–1862)

Classics:	Latin:	Sallust, Livy, or Ovid
	Greek:	Xenophon's *Cyropoedia,* or Homer
		Herodotus
		Greek and Roman Antiquities
		Greek and Roman Mythology (Manual of Classical Literature)
Mathematics:	Algebra (Loomis')	
	Elements of Geometry (Loomis', Six Books)	
English:	English Language	
	History and Composition	
Natural Science:	Physiology (Hitchcock's)	

Sophomore Course of Study (1862–1863)

Classics:	Latin:	Horace; Cicero—de Senecute, de Amicitia, de Natura Deorum
	Greek:	Xenophon's Memorabilia or Isocrates
		Select Plays of Euripides or Aeschylus
		Archaeology of Greek and Roman Literature
		History of Greek and Roman Literature

Archaeology of Art (Manual of Classical Literature)

Latin and Greek Exercises, and Written Translations

Mathematics: Geometry of Planes and Solids (Loomis')

Plane Trigonometry, Spherical Trigonometry (Loomis')

Navigation and Surveying (Loomis)

English: Political Economy (Wayland's)

Constitution of the United States (Sheppard's)

Mental Philosophy commenced (Hickok's)

Composition

Principles of Elocution (Caldwell's Manual)

Private Declamation

Natural Science: Physiology (finished)

Geology (Tenney's)

French: Fasquelle's Grammar

Voltaire's Charles XII or Dumas' Napoleon

Written Translations from English into French

Junior Course of Study (1863–1864)

Classics: Latin: Cicero de Officiis or Tusculan Disputations

Tacitus

Greek: Select Plays of Sophocles and Euripides

Demosthenes' Select Orations

Mathematics: Analytical Geometry continued

Differential and Integral Calculus, with applications
  (Loomis')

English: Mental Philosophy (completed)

Logic (Coppee's)

Rhetoric (Whately's)

Moral Science (Wayland's)

History (Weber's)

Public Declamation

Natural Science: Snell's Olmstead's Natural Philosophy

French: (Continued the first term), Scribe, Corneille or Moliere

Grammar Reviewed

Religion: Paley's Evidences

Greek Testament (the Historic Parts)

German: (The second term,) Woodbury's Grammar

Adler's Progressive Reader

Written Translations from English into German

Senior Course of Study (1864–1865)

Classics:	Latin:	Tacitus, Quintilian, Plautus or Juvenal
	Greek:	Select Plays of Aeschylus or Sophocles
		Plato or Aristotle
English:		History of Philosophy (Henry's)
		Public Declamation of Original Compositions
Mathematics:		Astronomy (Snell's Olmsted's)
Natural Science:		Chemistry (Johnston's Turner's)
		Lectures on Natural Philosophy and Chemistry
German:		Woodbury's Grammar (second half)
		Schiller's Tell, Goethe's Faust
		Written Translations from English into German
		Lectures on German Literature
Religion:		Moral Science (Wayland's)
		Butler's Analogy
		Greek Testament (the Epistles)

Summary of Expenses to Attend Dickinson College

BELOW ARE LISTS OF THE ANNUAL FEES PAID BY STUDENTS DURING Ashenfelter's four years at Dickinson College. As can be seen, the cost of attendance increased steadily during the four years of war, especially in Ashenfelter's senior year. The figures come from the *Catalogue of Dickinson College* for each academic year.

1861–1862
Tuition Fee: $33.00
Fee for Modern Languages: $3.00
Library Fee: $1.50
Use and warming of Recitation Rooms: $4.00
Janitor's Services: $3.00
Room Rent (Average): $9.00
Board, 40 weeks: $80.00 to $100.00 (Average $90.00)
Washing: $12.50
Fuel: $4.00
Lights: $7.00
Books, about: $15.00

1862–1863
Tuition Fee: $33.00
Fee for Modern Languages: $3.00
Library Fee: $1.50
Use and warming of Recitation Rooms: $5.00
Janitor's Services: $3.00

Room Rent (Average): $9.00
Board, 40 weeks: $80.00 to $110.00 (Average $100.00)
Washing: $12.50
Fuel: $6.00
Lights: $7.00
Books, about: $15.00

1863–1864
Tuition Fee: $33.00
Fee for Modern Languages: $3.00
Library Fee: $1.50
Use and warming of Recitation Rooms: $5.00
Janitor's Services: $3.00
Room Rent (Average): $9.00
Board, 40 weeks: $100.00 to $120.00 (Average $110.00)
Washing: $15.00
Fuel: $6.00
Lights: $7.50
Books, about: $15.00

Fig. 30. Photograph of Samuel Watts, the "sub janitor" at Dickinson College, taken by Charles F. Himes in February 1862. (Courtesy of the Library of Congress)

Fig. 29. Photograph of Henry Watts, an African American janitor at Dickinson College, taken by Charles F. Himes in February 1862. (Courtesy of the Library of Congress)

1864–1865

Tuition Fee: $40.00

Fee for Modern Languages: $5.00

Library Fee: $3.00

Use and warming of Recitation Rooms: $8.00

Janitor's Services: $5.00

Room Rent (Average): $11.00

Board, 40 weeks: $90.00 to $180.00 (Average $140.00)

Washing: $15.00

Fuel: $6.00

Lights: $7.50

Books, about: $25.00

Dickinson College during the Gettysburg Campaign

IN THE SUMMER OF 1863, DICKINSON COLLEGE EXPERIENCED THE CIVIL War firsthand. After Gen. Robert E. Lee's Army of Northern Virginia marched into Pennsylvania, Confederate troops occupied Carlisle June 27–30. The students "remained quietly at their posts," recalled Dr. Johnson in his 1864 report to the school's board of trustees, and "examinations proceeded in regular order." The president boasted that "while the community around us had been a prey to the intensest agitation," the students' "composure . . . displays the higher qualities of the philosopher. We feel that such young men can be trusted wherever duty shall call."[1]

Foregoing any formal commencement exercises, the graduating seniors were given their diplomas and "the blessing of the College," recalled Prof. Samuel D. Hillman. The students then quickly left by train "in the midst of alarms and wild rumors."[2] A few of the occupying rebels were familiar faces, some being Dickinson alumni. As a result, they took special care to leave the college unharmed. President Johnson's son, Theodore—who was nine years old at the time—later recalled that "not a thing of our's was destroyed, nor was the least bit of damage done to college property." During the occupation, hospitals were set up in campus buildings. While this was "but a temporary arrangement," noted Prof. John K. Stayman, it left a terribly unpleasant odor, and he looked forward to when "the smell of puddings and poultices coffee and castor-oil may no longer linger about the tower of the Muses, Classic Shades, Academic Groves, and all that sort of thing."[3]

1. James Henry Morgan, *Dickinson College: The History of One Hundred and Fifty Years, 1783–1933* (Carlisle, PA: Dickinson College, 1933), 314.

2. Samuel D. Hillman, "A Few Days under Rebel Rule," *Methodist*, July 18, 1863, DCA; Morgan, *Dickinson College*, 314–17.

3. John K. Stayman to Edgar E. Hastings, July [n.d.], Aug. 13, 1863, DCA.

Fig. 31. Prof. John K. Stayman. (Courtesy of Archives and Special Collections, Dickinson College, Carlisle, PA)

Some Carlisle residents despised having the rebels in their midst. Professor Hillman recalled them as a "dirty soldiery" who were commanded by "a proud, conceited, bombastic body of officers" and preached to by "canting and hypocritical rebel chaplains." But others had better interactions with the invaders. Dickinson alumnus Charles F. Himes noted that the rebels were "ragged and dirty" but also kind and civil. He even observed one Confederate officer consoling a crying girl who could not find her mother and later (with Dr. Johnson) had several "long chats" with Confederate officers.[4] Even Professor Hillman ended up showing some sympathy to the occupying force. Upon seeing a young soldier in want of shoes and with bleeding feet, he said, "It may be giving aid and comfort to the enemy, but, boy, I cannot stand the looks of those feet"; he then removed his own boots and gave them to the rebel.[5]

When the Confederates departed for Gettysburg on June 30, Union troops reoccupied Carlisle. On July 1, however, more Southern forces, led by Maj. Gen. J. E. B. Stuart, approached, this time warning the occupants that they would shell

4. Charles F. Himes (1838–1918) was the older brother of James Lanius Himes. He graduated from Dickinson in 1855 and returned to the college as a professor of natural science in 1865.

5. Hillman, "Few Days under Rebel Rule"; Charles F. Himes Pocket Diary, June 27, 1863, DCA; Conway W. Hillman to James H. Morgan, Sept. 9, 1930, DCA. Years later the soldier returned to Carlisle to thank Hillman for his kindness, telling him, "The boots were the greatest comfort I had had since leaving home."

Left: Fig. 32. Thomas M. Griffith, ca. 1858. (Courtesy of Archives and Special Collections, Dickinson College, Carlisle, PA)

Below: Fig. 33. Photograph of the homes of Profs. William C. Wilson and Samuel D. Hillman, taken by Charles F. Himes in February 1862. (Courtesy of the Library of Congress)

Fig. 34. This Thomas Nast engraving, *The Rebels Shelling the New York Militia in the Main Street of Carlisle, Pennsylvania,* appeared in *Harper's Weekly* on July 25, 1863. (Courtesy of Archives and Special Collections, Dickinson College, Carlisle, PA)

the town if they did not surrender. To this Maj. Gen. William F. "Baldy" Smith, the commanding officer of the Union force in Carlisle, replied, "Shell away and be damned!"[6] Stuart made good on his warning and, before any evacuation could be effected, commenced an artillery bombardment. Some residents—including Dickinson faculty—came outdoors with muskets to join the defending Union troops, most of whom were near Main Street. Among these were Professor Hillman and Rev. Francis J. Clerc, rector of St. John's Protestant Episcopal Church. "I saw men and women running into and behind the houses for safety, while the shot and shell flew through the streets and over the town," Hillman recalled.[7]

The bombardment continued for several hours, ending in the early morning of July 2. The town sustained a fair bit of damage, especially near Main Street. Among the damaged buildings was President Johnson's recitation room in East College, where an exploding shell "tore out several cubic yards of stone work, wrecked the woodwork; recitation benches, desks and tables being in one confused mass."[8]

6. Eric J. Wittenberg and J. David Petruzzi, *Plenty of Blame to Go Around: Jeb Stuart's Controversial Ride to Gettysburg* (New York: Savas Beattie, 2006), 141.

7. Hillman, "Few Days under Rebel Rule."

8. Morgan, *Dickinson College,* 316.

Alumnus Thomas M. Griffith (1834–98), class of 1858, sent a detailed account of what he saw to his siblings. From 1862 to 1864, Griffith served as the minister at Carlisle Emory Chapel.[9]

L. B. & M. A. Griffith
Carlisle, July 3, 1863

Dear Bro. & Sister

I suppose you have been quite anxious since you heard from me last. Communication was interrupted partly by the rebels, & partly from fear of them when their whereabouts was not known. Although our forces now occupy the place, the mail has not been opened up to Harrisburg. I hope to get this letter there by private individuals.

I wrote last on Wednesday June 24. That evening I met Dr. Johnson coming from the Hall who said there was no audience; the rumors of approaching rebels were so exciting that he thought they had better get the commencement closed next morning, & let the students go home. That night, people were removing their things into & through Carlisle, past my window. I was very busy till midnight, being on 2 or 3 committees, & had not finished examining papers & making out reports. The people in Carlisle itself did not seem much alarmed. I walked down about 11 o'clock & found but few in the streets. In the morning, at 8, the students & friends met in the college chapel, the degrees were conferred, & all finished for the year. At 10 most of the students left, but some stayed for several days & some are here yet. Next day, Friday, was very quiet, no rebels near to be found, we began to think they were not coming at all. But on Saturday about 10 o'clock we saw their advance guard on horseback coming into town, Gen. Jenkins[10] in command. In the afternoon the infantry came pouring in, the bands playing "Dixie's Land." One brigade occupied the campus front of my window. Gen. Ewell[11] commanded the whole, & had his headquarters at the garrison. There were about 7000, I think, though perhaps you heard there were 30000 or more. They were exceedingly orderly. Guards were placed to protect the college. I had removed my trunk & carpet-bag to the boarding house, & the best of my

9. Thomas M. Griffith to brother and sister, July 3, 1863, Thomas Miller Griffith Papers, MC 2005.4, DCA.

10. Confederate brigadier general Albert G. Jenkins (1830–64) commanded the 14th, 16th, 17th, 34th, and 36th Virginia Cavalry Regiments.

11. Confederate lieutenant general Richard S. Ewell (1817–72) became the commander of the Confederate 2nd Corps after Lt. Gen. Thomas Jonathan "Stonewall" Jackson was mortally wounded at the Battle of Chancellorsville in May 1863.

sermons to Prof. W.'s, but I soon found there was no cause for fear. I slept in my room as usual that night. The rebs were not allowed to touch private property; but their officers made a demand for rations, clothing & other stores. The rations were brought to the public square at noon, but for the rest they searched the stores. Those who had warehouses & groceries suffered most, but Confederate scrip or bonds were given. The scrip will bring 50 cts. on the dollar. They did not capture many horses for they were nearly all removed.

Our citizens made no resistence, except that on Thursday, some embankments were thrown up, & a few companies of citizens united with the garrison soldiers, in offering defense. But on Thursday night, orders from Harrisburg came, to fall back.

On Sunday, there was preaching in the campus by rebel chaplains. From my window, I could hear an occasional word. The former service lasted, I think nearly two hours. We had no service in our church. Some churches had; but Dr. Wing,[12] Mr. Black,[13] Mr. Clarc[14] & I concluded not to open our churches. Partly because I did not wish to appear like greeting the rebels & meeting them on friendly terms but rather to show our sense of the calamity by staying at home in silent grief; & partly because the rebels were so exceedingly dirty that they were not fit to enter any decent church. Their smell was offensive, their clothes ragged & filthy & moreover we could see that they were lousy.

They staid till Tuesday morning at 5, when they left, apparently in haste, as if they had heard bad news. Several of our students whom I knew were among them, J. J. White[15] (whose likeness you have was one of the captains)[.] I had some talk with him, but did not care about meeting any of them with any cordiality. I heard that Findlay,[16] Cloud,[17] & Effinger[18] were here also; & others I saw.

---

12. Rev. Conway P. Wing (1809–89) was minister of the First Presbyterian Church of Carlisle. He earned his doctor of divinity at Dickinson College in 1857.

13. Rev. R. W. Black was the minister of Allison United Methodist Church in Carlisle from 1863 to 1864.

14. Rev. Francis J. Clerc (1823–1907) was rector of St. John's Protestant Episcopal Church.

15. John Josiah White (1836–94) of Loudon County, Virginia, was a member of the class of 1858.

16. Frank Smith Findlay (1834–1905) of Abingdon, Virginia, was a member of the class of 1857. He entered the Confederate army as a private in the 1st Virginia Cavalry in 1861. In 1861 and 1862 he served as a courier for General Stuart, later becoming a captain in the 4th Virginia State Line. He was wounded in Kentucky on December 4, 1862, and, as a consequence, would not have been present for the Confederate invasion of Pennsylvania. After the war Findlay returned to Virginia, where he practiced law.

17. Daniel Mountjoy Cloud (1837–71) of Warren County, Virginia, was a member of the class of 1857 or 1858 but did not graduate. During the war, he served in Ashby's Cavalry from 1861 to

On Tuesday forenoon, about 60 of our men were brought in as prisoners, to the public square. A guard of rebels was placed over them, their shoes were taken by the rebs. The ladies soon brought bread & meat, butter, jelly, jams, cherry pies &c. &c. The young men threw tobacco to them, & after they were paroled the citizens took them to their houses & supplied their wants.

In the evening Jenkins' Cavalry (or mounted infantry) occupied the campus again; but only till about 11 o'clock that night. In the morning all the rebels had left & by afternoon our troops from Harrisburg occupied the town. Provisions in abundance were brought to the square, & about 6000 of our men ate their suppers there. They met with a hearty welcome. It was reported that the rebels were driven back & our troops expected to meet them either in the town or a few miles out, but soon the excitement died away.

But about 8 o'clock, the cavalry of Fitz Hugh Lee,[19] came into town (about 2000 strong so far as I can find out) & took our men by surprise while some were eating; but they sprang to their arms & returned their fire vigorously. I was sitting on Prof. Wilson's portico at the time, along with Mr Clarke,[20] Miss Walraven,[21] & Miss Johnson.[22] We heard the fire of musketry, & afterward the whizzing of

---

1863, then as a captain in the Confederate Secret Service. Following the war, he settled in Vicksburg, Mississippi, where he was superintendent of public schools and then an attorney.

18. William Henry Effinger (1839–1909), a member of the class of 1858, served as an officer in the 11th Virginia Cavalry. Following the war, he moved out west, settling in Portland, Oregon, where he practiced law.

19. Confederate brigadier general Fitzhugh Lee (1835–90) was a nephew of Gen. Robert E. Lee.

20. Asbury Jones Clarke (1841–1907) of Shirleysburg, Pennsylvania, was a member of the class of 1863. He later became a lawyer and trustee of the college. In 1918 his widow endowed the Asbury J. Clarke Chair of Latin in his honor.

Clarke and Prof. William C. Wilson appear to have been quite close. Later in 1863, when Clarke was drafted, Wilson wrote to him explaining that he would not be able to get out of the draft by claiming Carlisle as his residence. "The act provides specially that [students] shall be enrolled at the place of residence of their parents," he wrote. "So you see that loophole is stopped & you cant escape your duty. So prepare to shoulder your knapsack or 'fork over' your greenbacks." (This was a reference to the law's provision that draftees could avoid service by paying a $300 commutation fee.) William C. Wilson to Asbury J. Clarke, Sept. 17, 1863, collection of Jonathan W. White.

21. Mary Ann "Annie" Walraven, a sister or sister-in-law of Professor Wilson who lived in his household, became the guardian of Wilson's son and daughter when the professor died on March 2, 1865. According to Augusta Lutie Johnson, daughter of Dickinson College president Herman M. Johnson, Wilson's death was a "severe shock to her nerves" and caused Walraven to have "several severe fainting spells." Lutie to Asbury J. Clarke, Mar. 13, 1865, collection of Jonathan W. White.

22. Lutie Johnson had just turned twenty years old on June 27.

2 or 3 shells over the town. Miss J. & Mr C. left for Dr. Johnson's, & we stood at the gate. Soon some citizens came along saying our men had driven the rebels back. Then there was quiet for a time. Miss Walraven had the house locked & the children removed, & we went to Dr. J's. Some wounded were brought in to West College (which is now the hospital) I gave one of my mattresses some comforts, pillow &c. Soon the firing & shelling commenced again. One shell struck the college, tore a corner of the wall off at a window, entered Dr. J's lecture room, tore an opposite door off its hinges, & scattered the stones & dust all over the floors (the shell was found, & part will be put in the college museum, as a relic of this instance of southern barbarity) shells struck different buildings about town, but none of the citizens were hurt. We stayed together in the basement & cellar, where we were safe. At one time Miss Walraven & Mr. Clarke went out to see after Prof. W's children whom we had left at a neighbor's house. Coming back a shell burst over them. On entering, Miss W. fainted but soon recovered. The shelling was kept up at intervals till 3 o'clock in the morning, but a great part of the time, there was no firing. The rebs sent a flag of truce 3 times demanding surrender but Gen. Smith[23] always refused. Dr. & I went to see Gen. Smith at midnight to ask if any time was allowed for removing the women & children. He said there was none given by the rebels, except that at first they said the women & chn should leave before they commenced shelling a second time, but had made no arrangement for cessation of hostilities. About 2 o'clock Dr. roused us up (we were lying on the floor) saying he thought we had better leave for at daylight the shelling would be apt to commence again. I opposed it, saying I thought we were safer where we were. We concluded to stay, but there was very little sleeping done. A few shells were thrown at 3 o'clock but after that all was quiet.

The rebels burned the garrison & gas house, & in the morning all left. Our wounded numbered 17, or less. I often go over to see them in the college where they are. I am very glad I stayed to see all this & am quite contented, safe & well. This is my post & I did not feel like leaving it. We have had no papers nor letters for a week.

TMG

---

23. Union major general William F. "Baldy" Smith (1824–1903).

Ashenfelter's 1864 Speech, "Capital Punishment"

ON JUNE 27, 1864, ASHENFELTER DELIVERED AN ORATION ENTITLED "Capital Punishment" as part of the Junior Prize Contest at Dickinson College. As described in his letter of late February 1865, he purposefully botched his delivery in order to persuade Alice Rheem that he would not be successful enough in life to support her. He earned ninety-eight out of one hundred points for the written paper but only forty-nine for his delivery. This speech may be the only surviving example of Ashenfelter's college work and gives a sense of the sort of assignment Dickinson students were required to complete during the Civil War years. Moreover, it provides a glimpse into how Ashenfelter portrayed himself to his peers and faculty, alluding to God in this public statement at the same time he was writing to Pennypacker about his atheism.

. . .

In man's nature, the Social Element is characterized by a peculiar power. Its influence has been strikingly exhibited in almost every variety of association. All records of the past, as well as all knowledge of the present establish indisputably the strength of the bond by which man is united with his fellow.

Barbaric tribes those first attempts at human organization, proved, at an early stage of the world's history, to be insufficient for the grand purpose of human advancement. The world *felt* the meaning of that word—progress; but before this feeling could be developed into organized action, old predjudices were to be eradicated—old associations to be dissolved. To this end war was the great instrument. As an individual, man felt his insecurity; when associated, his safety; & with the dictates of nature supported by self interest, a necessity was recognized, & the individual rapidly became merged into the nation. Coincident with the perception of national association as essential to individual safety arose a recognized tendency to human advancement. Governments began to establish law as necessary to their own regulation, as safeguards against themselves. In this justice was to be greatly regarded. It would in effect have defeated the object of unity should the individuals thus associated have been compelled, in their very organization, to subject themselves to a danger approaching that which they had sought to avoid. The world's welfare demanded that governmental authority should be limited, & hence arose the question, how far does the jurisdiction of human government extend? It is a strange fact that the popular voice has placed absolutely no limit upon this law power. The world has moved on through these thousands of years of progress without once attempting to cast off that fearful influence which association holds over its component individuals.

In inquiring as to the justice of capital punishment, it is hardly necessary to refer to the original rights of the persons associated. For although the object of government is retarded, if not entirely defeated by the life power of the individual collective over the individual component, yet, from the nature of justice itself the truths are sufficiently evidenced. When the application is personal, we recognize the inestimable value of existence. By the principles of association, society is thrown into what is essentially the position of an individual. Occupying such position, it claims to find a justification for the punishment of death in the principle of self defense. And yet, we find that the application of this principle to society differs widely from its application to the individual. For in the one, it is almost unlimited; while in the other, it is justified only by certain external circumstances. The one claims power over the life of the offender, even when the danger to itself is slight, & when other means of avoidance are immediately at hand. To the other, the right arises from immediate danger to self existence & can be exercised only when all other means have proved inadequate. Here then, is an essential difference; & here, a glaring inconsistency. Society by its own regulation places itself in a position which, when occupied by the individual, by that same regulation becomes criminal. But whence is the right derived? Is man's accountability to society higher than Society's to God? Has association, standing as an individual, a right to make punishment of crime identical with crime itself and thus practically deny its accountability to a higher power. No *one* man can, in justice, deprive another of existence, nor can *any* specified number; & the right which is denied the individual cannot be given to association. The great theory is that each man consents to give up certain of his natural rights for the good of the whole:—that the control of his actions, which belongs originally to himself, is entrusted to some superior power, called sovereignty or government. But this is *only* theory. For each man, instead of acting voluntarily, finds himself at his birth in a state of subjection, & to submit is a necessity. We shudder at the horrors of bigoted superstition. But where is the essential difference between the principle which ordered the action of inquisition & that which sways modern government? The former, claiming that ultimate purpose justified present means and with the world's spiritual regeneration as an object, held and exercised the power over human life & death; the latter occupies the same position on the ground of self interest. No one hesitates for a moment in stamping the former as fearfully wrong. Why then, attempt a justification of the latter? Evidently, it is but a modern application of the old principle that ends justify means.

Again, the spirit with which an act is committed does not affect the justice or injustice of the abstract act. The palliation of an offender does not justify offense. We claim that to kill is of itself essentially wrong. And that a wrong never becomes a right merely because it can be made to serve some advantageous end. If deprivation of life is not, of itself, a crime, then the criminality rests with surrounding circumstances; and a man is deserving of punishment when found to be in a position in which he might kill. Evidently then, government is most absurdly inconsistent. For, by the very act of punishment, it declares murder a crime; & so declaring, murders in order that crime may cease.

In civilized society, the first & principal incentives to all action should be justice & goodness. The welfare of an offender should not be allowed to pass unregarded. Evidently, the advantage accruing to society may be as well obtained through other means—through means which might be productive of much good to the criminal. We recognize his reformation as the first great object of punishment. We see the principle exemplified in the incidents of everyday life. It has formed a part of our own personal experience. No one would claim that a parent punishes an offending child [with] any other object than that child's benefit. And here is the natural, here the principal aim. Clearly, this reformation of the offender would be advantageous to society. But yet, how utterly absurd are the means employed for this good end. The one so much needing improvement, the hardened criminal, with the blood of his victim yet red upon his hands, with his heart steeled by hatred, & his moral faculties deadened by passion, is hurried to death. His reformation set at naught, & the first great object of punishment entirely defeated.

But it is needless to continue. We claim that human life is inviolable—that the deliberate destruction of the exquisite mechanism of our bodily existence cannot be in accordance with the great & good designs of our beneficent creator. Man was never endowed with the vital principle as a temptation to his fellow.

I thank God that this is an age of progress—that the relics of old barbarism are being eradicated. Christianity is urging the world forward. From the enlightened truths of revealed religion arises a new era. The past has been fearfully dark, but the world needed experience. As christianity & civilization move forward, the world will awaken to a fearful knowledge of its self licensed criminality. From the dawning brightness of this present, which we grasp here,—which we are experiencing, spring hopes of a glorious future. Let us, then, look forward in all the enjoyment of these high anticipations. Let us so order our actions that when the bright hour does come, we may enjoy the happy consciousness of having labored for the right.

Index

"*The Most Complete Political Machine Ever Known*": *The North's Union Leagues in the American Civil War* · Paul Taylor

A Family and Nation under Fire: The Civil War Letters and Journals of William and Joseph Medill · Edited by Georgiann Baldino

Untouched by the Conflict: The Civil War Letters of Singleton Ashenfelter, Dickinson College · Edited by Jonathan W. White and Daniel Glenn